MAKE
YOUR MARK

—

THE 99U
BOOK SERIES

—

Manage Your Day-to-Day:
*Build Your Routine, Find Your Focus,
and Sharpen Your Creative Mind*

Maximize Your Potential:
*Grow Your Expertise, Take Bold Risks,
and Build an Incredible Career*

Make Your Mark:
*The Creative's Guide to Building a
Business with Impact*

MAKE YOUR MARK

The Creative's Guide to Building a Business with Impact

—

Edited by Jocelyn K. Glei
Foreword by Scott Belsky

Published by Amazon Publishing, Seattle

www.apub.com

Amazon, the Amazon logo, and Amazon Publishing are trademarks of Amazon.com,
Inc. or its affiliates.

ISBN-10: 1477801235
ISBN-13: 9781477801239

For the Makers

WHAT IS 99U?

—

For too long, the creative world has focused on idea generation at the expense of idea execution. As the legendary inventor Thomas Edison famously said, "Genius is 1 percent inspiration, and 99 percent perspiration." To make great ideas a reality, we must act, experiment, fail, adapt, and learn on a daily basis.

99U is Behance's effort to provide this "missing curriculum" for making ideas happen. Through our Webby Award–winning website, popular events, and bestselling books, we share pragmatic, action-oriented insights from leading researchers and visionary creatives.

At 99U, we don't want to give you more ideas—we want to empower you to make good on the ones you've got.

PREFACE

—

What do Dropbox, Nest, Uber, and Airbnb all have in common? Each began as a two- or three-man start-up operation that has been transformed, in seven years or less, from a small idea into a serious business—with a multibillion-dollar valuation to boot. When you step back and look at lightning-fast growth trajectories like these, it's clear that the rules of business have changed. Many of the classic tenets that have guided great companies for decades are now outmoded or irrelevant at best.

To craft companies that can thrive in this fast-paced, e-commerce-driven, socially connected world, we need a new playbook—one that reflects the values and the strategies of this new breed of creative business. To create just that with *Make Your Mark*, we went straight to the source, tapping twenty-one leading experts and entrepreneurs for their insights on what's new and different about building a business right now.

To share just a sampling: Warby Parker co-founder Neil Blumenthal explains why customers' BS detectors are more sensitive than ever (and what that means for building a brand), Google X's Sebastian Thrun discusses the importance of relentless iteration and fast failure, Buffer founder Joel Gascoigne articulates the unexpected benefits of adopting a policy of radical transparency, and Facebook's Julie Zhuo makes the case for an approach to product design that's so simple and streamlined it's almost invisible.

As the book came together, I noticed certain themes bubbling up again and again that epitomized the core values of this new guard of creative entrepreneurs. And, refreshingly, they aren't about money or profit—despite the billion-dollar examples mentioned above—but rather about making an impact. I observed a renewed commitment to craftsmanship and the desire to create truly beautiful product experiences, a powerful focus on the importance of both giving and serving (your customers and your team), and a fierce dedication to building businesses that will change the world for the better.

Whether you're about to launch a new company or are considering how to retool an existing business, my hope is that this collection will offer you fresh thinking, practical advice, and the moxie to get out there and make something that matters.

— JOCELYN K. GLEI, editor-in-chief, 99U

TABLE
OF
CONTENTS
–

BUILDING YOUR PRODUCT

SERVING YOUR CUSTOMERS

LEADING YOUR TEAM

Coda: A CALL TO ACTION

MAKING AN IMPACT IN WHAT MATTERS MOST TO YOU

—

Scott Belsky, Founder of Behance and Author of Making Ideas Happen

Creativity has many definitions.

For me, creativity is solving problems in new ways and conceiving new ways of looking at the world.

Creativity can be expressed in many forms, like art, science, and thought.

But creativity is all too often undiscoverable and incomprehensible.

Art, without distribution and discovery, moves nobody. Did it ever exist? Science, without clear explanation and advocacy, won't be understood by the masses. Will it make an impact?

Thought, if not written down and shared with others, changes nothing. Does it matter?

Your ideas, if not captured and executed, affect nobody. Are they relevant?

Creation must be made accessible for consumption. This is your real job.

Execution, distribution, packaging, marketing, messaging, strategy, leadership . . . this is business.

Without great management and stewardship, creativity—like fireworks—will flash and then dim to dust.

The potential of creativity—and your ability to sustain yourself and serve others through creativity—is more about business than it is about ideas.

This book is about applying the forces of business to creativity. It's not about making money; it's about making an impact.

It's about channeling, packaging, and delivering your talent for others to consume it.

It's also about scaling your talent for more people to benefit from it. With creativity comes a drive to succeed.

But unlike traditional measures of success—like money, titles, or status—the creative mind is driven by a desire to see creativity come to life. Success is making an impact in what matters most to you.

To make an impact with creativity, you must love what you do.

Otherwise, don't bother. It requires too many hours of hardship, self-doubt, and pain to conceive of something new and birth it into the world. It takes struggle that you genuinely believe is worth the pain. You must do it as a labor of love.

To keep at it long enough to become exceptional, your labor must be sustainable. You must learn to earn a living with your art (or science or thought) so that you can nourish yourself as you nourish your work.

In this third book in 99U's "missing curriculum" for creative leaders, we dive into creativity as a business. From defining your purpose and the problem you're solving to building products that serve people, how do you set yourself up to make an impact in what matters most to you?

The book ahead is our attempt to outfit you for creativity as a business. If you don't manage your ideas like an entrepreneur, they will die with you. Jump in and take the reins.

CHAPTER ONE

DEFINING

YOUR

PURPOSE

–

*How to uncover your mission
in the world and define your
modus operandi*

The first thing to understand about building an incredible business is that it's not about you. Well, it's not ONLY about you. Rather, it's about finding the perfect alignment between your specific talents and expertise and what the world needs.

That's why the best businesses aren't profit-driven or even product-driven; they're purpose-driven. They strive to solve real problems, meet pressing needs, and change the world in ways big and small. They make a commitment to constantly learning and iterating and evolving to become better at executing their missions. They focus on creating value, and let everything else follow.

Thus we begin this book with a deep inquiry—composed of insights, ideas, and questions—into how to discover your purpose and stay true to it throughout the life of your business. Moving beyond the simplistic, get-rich-quick, start-up narrative, we'll look at how to create something with meaning for you—and for your customers.

Because, at the end of the day, it's not about building up your ego or nailing the next massive IPO; it's about making something that matters.

FINDING YOUR PURPOSE
AND LIVING IT

—

Keith Yamashita

Certain people exude such a powerful presence
that they can absolutely captivate you within the
very first moment of meeting them. When I was
introduced to Bill Thomas at a conference, he
was that kind of mesmerizing. A fortysomething,
Harvard-trained doctor casually dressed in jeans
and Birkenstocks, he took the stage and spoke
passionately—with an actor's eloquence—about aging.

He laid out a vast and ambitious plan for how America could trans-
form the experience of growing older, of what it means to be well, and
of how we care for people in their seventies, eighties, and nineties.

He argued that the medical system, the elder-care system, and the nursing home system have to evolve: "Aging should be conceived of as an era of continual growth and renewal, rather than a period of decline," he said. He had absolute clarity in every part of his argument, and his energy was both motivating and mobilizing.

When I talked to him after his session, I asked, "Bill, how do you describe your purpose in life?" He answered, spontaneously and effortlessly, "To bring respect back to elderhood in America." In eight words, he captured his entire life's work. Bill reminded me that the first step in living your purpose is to distill it. This very act sets an accurate compass heading. It shapes your choices, tells you what is important, and helps you separate the merely interesting from the truly crucial.

HOW TO FIND YOUR COMPANY'S PURPOSE

So how might you go about finding your purpose in a way that's as compelling as Bill's? How do you find a due north course for yourself, or your tribe, or your entire company—a course that you may sometimes veer from, but that always draws you back to center?

Over the years, I've worked with leaders from Apple, IBM, Nike, Facebook, and numerous other companies on making this journey. As we begin to imagine—or reimagine—the company's purpose, the process typically begins with looking at the intersection of several key truths:

- What does the world hunger for? What does it desire? What does it need or suffer from a lack of?

- What are the unique talents of the organization?

- Who has the company timelessly been?

- And who must it fearlessly become?

A company's purpose lies at the center of these four forces.

To discover it, we incite debate, storytelling, self-examination, study sessions in the historical archives, musings about the future. We help leaders in these companies find what they truly care about.

That work of introspection and getting to clarity is rarely easy. But it is almost always rewarding. Once defined, purpose informs a company's every move. It adds meaning and mindfulness to day-to-day operations and motivation that goes far beyond.

HOW TO FIND YOUR PERSONAL PURPOSE

What's interesting is that this method, which works so well for finding a compass heading for a company, also works for individuals. To define your personal purpose, start with these questions:

- How will the world be better off thanks to you having been on this earth?

- What are your unique gifts and superpowers?

- Who have you been when you've been at your best?

- Who must you fearlessly become?

At the intersection of these four questions lies your personal purpose.

The questions are deceptively simple, and you might be tempted to rush through them. To really do the task justice—and to do yourself justice—you have to peel away the layers of your self-conception. You have to get beyond that image you've made for yourself that you so strongly defend. And you have to get at what is actually true. The tension among your answers reveals as much as the commonalities. Lean into it. This process may take days. It may obsess your thinking for weeks. For some, it takes years to unfold. There is no magical timeline. Move at your own pace.

The same process holds true whether you're a leader doing the hard work of articulating a purpose for your organization or you're an individual ready to live a more directed life.

$$\sim\!\!\infty\!\!\sim$$

So let me return to my story about Bill Thomas. At the end of our conversation, he said to me, "What would you say your purpose is, Keith?" I thought about it a bit, then started to talk: "I work with companies as they go through deep, formative periods of transformation. I work with CEOs to help mobilize people during those times of change. Along the way, I help them see things from new vantage points, and then help those institutions rise to the challenge ..." I kept talking, but Bill politely interrupted. "Keith, way too much! It doesn't sound like you're very clear about what your personal purpose is."

I was stumped. His reaction made me reflect.

I consider myself a fairly self-aware and mindful person (don't we all?), and I thought I was pretty clear about why I've been put on this earth.

But Bill pointed out something powerful. The work of introspection is put into action only once you've succinctly put your purpose into words.

After leaving the conference, I spent a few weeks crafting what I believe my purpose is. "To help people aspire, then be, great." And then, coincidentally—or perhaps there are no true coincidences—99U asked me to write this essay.

PUTTING PURPOSE INTO ACTION

Once you've vocalized your unique purpose, how exactly does it play out? How do you put it into action?

I like the way Richard Leider, one of the world's foremost experts on purpose, describes how to approach the next step. He defines purpose as being in the right place with the people who matter to you, doing your life's work. So the endeavor becomes, in Richard's words, to "pack" and "repack" one's life—discarding ideas, thoughts, duties, old baggage about relationships, in favor of packing the things you truly need to be at your best in life.

I am constantly humbled at how purpose drives the people and companies I admire:

Casey Sheahan served as the CEO of outdoor clothing pioneer Patagonia for a decade. In his post, he was responsible not only for the financial health of the company but also for charting its positive impact in the world. His personal purpose is about helping people live a mindful existence—that is, to bring thoughtfulness and intentionality to their work and play. Meanwhile, Patagonia's purpose is to "build the best product, cause no unnecessary harm, and use business to inspire and implement solutions to the environmental crisis." With both his personal and business purposes aligned, Casey created a company culture that continues to make Patagonia the proof of concept for a different kind of compassionate business.

Ask: *How can your personal purpose align with your organization's purpose to create the conditions to do good in the world?*

Bill McDonough—the sui generis thinker behind the cradle-to-cradle design approach—demonstrates a commitment to his personal purpose of creating a sustainable planet in how feverishly he lives it out. He crisscrosses the globe. He's in China one day helping to build sustainable cities, and speaking to young architects about how to rethink energy efficiency on the next. One day he's with the CEO of Ford Motor Company discussing different kinds of transportation, and the next he's researching the chemical composition of building materials to create ones that are healthy for the planet.

Ask: *Can you live your purpose in a more all-encompassing way?*

Artist, architect, and activist Maya Lin's purpose shows up not only in what she makes but also in what she chooses not to make. She spends her time focused solely on the projects and causes that allow her to grow and contribute. She says "no" to the rest. Restraint and discipline come to those who are clear about their purpose in life.

-

Ask: *What does your purpose reveal about what you should stop doing?*

In the start-up realm of Silicon Valley, companies live or die by how quickly they move and act. But for Dave Morin—one of Facebook's most impactful early employees and today the founder of mobile social network Path—smart is more important than fast. In order to help his company live up to its purpose of creating technologies that bring us closer to the people we love, he has started a "slow product movement"—a mindful practice that is not about speed of product development but the quality of the things he develops.

-

Ask: *What does your purpose imply you must be patient about?*

PURPOSE DRIVES IMPACT, IMPACT REWARDS PURPOSE

Purpose compels you to act. It brings into focus the things that matter most.

I asked Bill Thomas how he's made so many strides in advancing his cause over the years. His response: "I entertain the conversations, meetings, relationships that are most in line with my purpose over any other activity. Frankly, life is simply too short to fritter away your time chasing things that don't matter to you. Or to the world."

And here is the most interesting bit: The impact you have in the world also affirms your purpose. Impact justifies purpose. It fuels purpose. It empowers you to live your purpose more boldly every day.

This is how everyday people can achieve extraordinary things. We listen to that purpose. We achieve things because of our purpose. And that in turn makes each of us hungry to live by our purpose even more. In our own humble way, this is how people become great.

Will you take the next step? Will you invest the time to find your personal purpose? Will you gather your colleagues to define the purpose of your organization? In that move, greatness emerges.

KEITH YAMASHITA *is the founder and chairman of SY—a consultancy and product-creation engine dedicated to helping companies, teams, and individuals be great. He's collaborated with CEOs and leadership teams at companies like Apple, eBay, IBM, GE, Nike, and Starbucks, and he speaks and writes about leadership, design, and transformation.*

→ www.sypartners.com

"Find out who you are,

and do it on purpose."

— DOLLY PARTON

BECOMING A LEAN, MEAN, LEARNING MACHINE

—

Aaron Dignan

In the early days of a new business, you make choices—conscious and unconscious—that will influence your culture far into the future. If you're not careful, those choices can become patterns that limit your ability to thrive. Consider that today's most trusted and important institutions—in business, health care, government, philanthropy, and beyond—are struggling to stay relevant and useful in the face of new entrants and rapid change. It's as if they were wired for a completely different environment.

For the past seven years, my team and I have been studying the fastest growing, most profoundly impactful organizations of our time.

What we've found is that these companies exhibit a new way of working—a new organizational operating system (OS). We call this new system a Responsive OS, as it affords these companies greater responsiveness to competition, culture, technology, and all other forms of disruption.

Responsive organizations may start small (like Warby Parker or Quirky), but they have the potential to get bigger fast (like Airbnb, Tesla, Uber, Dropbox, Evernote, Square, and Jawbone), and ultimately dominate markets (like Amazon, Google, Twitter, Facebook, and PayPal).

What's different about these companies is that they are lean, mean, learning machines. They have an intense bias to action and a high tolerance for risk, expressed through frequent experimentation and relentless product iteration. They hack together products and services, test them, and improve them, while their legacy competition edits project plans in PowerPoint. They are obsessed with company culture and top-tier talent, with an emphasis on employees that can imagine, build, and test their own ideas. They are hypersensitive to friction—in their daily operations and their user experiences. They are open, connected, and build with, and for, their communities of users and co-conspirators. They are comfortable with the unknown; business models and customer value are revealed over time. And most importantly, they are driven by a purpose greater than just profit; each is explicit about how they intend to change the world in some small (or utterly massive) way.

When you consider the speed with which these companies enter and dominate markets, it's clear that organizations everywhere need to upgrade their OS or they risk extinction. Whether you're a freelancer with aspirations of building the next great brand or the CEO of a publicly traded company—that means you.

CORE VALUES OF THE RESPONSIVE OS

Think of your OS as the sum total of all the values, processes, and methods inside your organization. If the business plan is the "what" of the org, the OS is the "why" and "how." Put another way, it's your organizational DNA. Companies that know who they are (i.e., have a strong OS) have an easier time translating their brand into new categories and contexts. That's why we can picture Apple making a car or Google venturing into health care; they bring with them a codified "way of working" that will define how they approach that new space.

What our research has revealed is that all responsive organizations share a handful of common values that will define the next age of business. Their legacy competitors, meanwhile, have an opposing set of values that are limiting their ability to survive and thrive. As we contrast these differing approaches to running a company, consider how they may be expressed in your business practices, and how you can implement responsive values in your future decisions.

Visionary vs. Commercial

Legacy businesses tend to focus on commercial outcomes: to be the number one player in a market or hit an earnings target. For them, success is about business performance. But for responsive companies, vision and impact are paramount. Making a "dent in the universe" trumps anything else they might achieve. Everything they do, including financial success, is in service of that goal.

Tip: Pick a vision that is ambitious and far-reaching enough to last decades, not years. Commit everything to your cause. Ensure that tough decisions are purpose-driven, especially when it hurts.

Lean vs. Large

The last age of business was defined in part by an intense desire for growth. Before the age of software, it took a lot of people to scale a business, so growth came primarily from geographic and market expansion. Efficiencies of scale and barriers to entry meant that having a huge sales force or a massive R&D team were valuable assets. The cost of that scale, however, has been a loss of speed, agility, and simplicity. The new guard prizes leanness in every aspect of operations, from team size to project budgets.

-

Tip: Commit to lean business practices that will keep you honest as you scale. Use strategies such as two-pizza teams, short iterative development cycles, weekly scrums, and funding that is unlocked through user validation.

Open vs. Closed

In decades past, the core value of legacy institutions was isolation—closed doors, offices, silos, departments, and secret innovation processes. One of the major shifts of the digital age has been pervasive connectivity—to each other and to every piece of information ever created. What this has revealed is a far more complex system, with countless overlapping constituents, where real value is often at the intersection of unplanned encounters and collaborations. Information is still power, but it's more powerful when it is shared and permeates boundaries. In a Responsive OS, value is placed on transparency, connections, and community. This gives birth to open innovation, tightly knit cultures, and a greater collective intelligence.

-

Tip: *Demand a culture of transparent communication. Use new tools to ensure that this is possible, even when team members are working remotely. When in doubt, choose to be open—with your plans, your product, and your data.*

Learning vs. Sustaining

Once you become successful, you almost certainly have something to lose, and the natural instinct is to protect that success. Large legacy businesses tend to have this attitude. They are naturally risk averse because they have so much to lose. Meanwhile, start-ups and smaller competitors with nothing to lose are willing to bet the farm on innovations, take risks, and even fail, in pursuit of the best possible solution for a market. And enough of them hit home runs every year to shape and reshape the world around us. Whatever the size of your company, adopting a Responsive OS means that you view every activity as a chance to learn and refine your process. Success means never settling for what worked in the past.

-

Tip: *Adopt agile principles and processes wherever possible. Define "survivable risk" and make sure every employee knows what it* *looks like. As you achieve some measure of success, switch to a bimodal strategy of improving your current products while placing wild bets on new ones.*

Emergent vs. Controlled

Legacy organizations tend to operate cultures that maintain tight control of the empire. Because of their sheer size, bureaucracy and hierarchy have become natural reflexes. They are used to being able to reach out and shape the world—and their customers—at will. They don't let things happen; they make things happen. Responsive companies, by contrast, are comfortable with a lot more uncertainty. This manifests in many ways. First, they let their org structure morph and shape-shift to reflect the nature of the work at hand. Roles are fluid. People wear many hats. Further, they let products and platforms find their true purpose in collaboration with their users; as the product is used (and misused), the feedback loop is open. Twitter, for instance, did not know it was going to disrupt the news media. That future was allowed to emerge. Firms with a Responsive OS rely on an intuition about where to dig but not what they might find. They are open to the possibilities and all the upside that comes with them.

-

Tip: *Let your org structure reveal itself, and pick a method for allowing your company to adapt its structure and processes over time. Start new projects with intuition, letting customer input and user behavior shape your products and services over time.*

Legacy behavior is the natural by-product of scale and success, and, as such, we are all susceptible to it. As your business grows and thrives, the greatest lesson from this generation of responsive organizations may well be the notion that we must "upgrade" our approaches and behaviors on a regular basis—tweaking sources of tension, adapting to new technologies, and releasing new versions of ourselves constantly.

AARON DIGNAN is the CEO of Undercurrent, where he advises global brands and complex organizations like GE, American Express, PepsiCo, the Bill & Melinda Gates Foundation, Ford Motor Company, and Cooper-Hewitt on how to become more responsive to an ever-changing world.

→ www.undercurrent.com

"No matter what, expect the unexpected.

And whenever possible, BE the unexpected."

— LYNDA BARRY

Q&A:

LAUNCHING IDEAS THAT WILL CHANGE THE WORLD

—

with Tim O'Reilly

The evolution of the Internet as we know it today owes a huge debt to Tim O'Reilly. From Web 2.0 to the open-source and maker movements, O'Reilly has demonstrated a remarkable ability to help ideas take off by giving them "a local habitation and name." Both an investor and an entrepreneur, O'Reilly also founded O'Reilly Media, whose books and events have played a key role in the spread of programming languages and technology-driven ideas. We talked to O'Reilly about how ideas turn into movements and the power of getting really, really excited about changing the world.

Where do you think great business ideas come from?

Innovation starts with enthusiasts. The reason why it starts with enthusiasts is that they are focused on the right priority, which is the change they want to make in the world, versus say, a business idea that will get funded. Their perspective is: How cool would it be if we could all have our own computers? How cool would it be if I could put up information for free on the Internet and anybody could access it? How cool would it be if I could build an assistive robot for my grandmother?

What should entrepreneurs be thinking about if they really want to make an impact?

Aaron Levie of Box tweeted something great about Uber recently. He said, "Uber is a $3.5 billion lesson in building for how the world should work instead of optimizing for how the world does work."

Being able to see the world in a fresh way is the essence of being an entrepreneur. You have an idea about the way the world ought to be. You have a theory about why and how you are going to connect the dots.

I was just in a meeting with a very interesting nonprofit entrepreneur who is having trouble getting her ideas accepted, and I think it's really a failure of user focus. You need to know who is your customer; who cares about this? Identifying that community of people who care and having a deep understanding of why they care is so central.

It could be as simple as a subset of people and you understand what they want in a way that maybe they have not even understood themselves yet.

Let's say that you've identified this community and this thing that they do not yet know they want. How do you get them to understand that they want it?

I believe in the power of storytelling. We live in a world of stories that are really our maps to how to think about the world. People who succeed in that kind of storytelling are telling what I would call "emotionally intelligent stories."

I was having breakfast with a woman recently, and she made the comment that the NRA is an emotionally intelligent organization. I thought that was extremely interesting. I'm not sure that I would refer to the organization in that way, but it's absolutely right that they have figured out what the hot-button emotional issue is for a specific subset of people.

For me, creating emotionally intelligent stories is about listening and persisting. You keep telling the story and you pull a thread and if it doesn't break you pull a little harder and . . . Well, it's not exactly rocket science. Then again, it's not easy, either.

It seems like you've really used the power of language to mobilize people around ideas over

the years. You find that key turn of phrase that helps them hang on to the idea, process it, and make it their own.

That's true. With movements like "Web 2.0" or "open source," there was already a movement, but until there was a name to unify the movement, it couldn't reach its full potential. I saw the possibility of activating the communities that those names represented and giving them a way to present themselves to the world that was newly meaningful.

A big piece of what I try to do is to help names like these do a better job of telling the truth. What I mean by "the truth" is you build a map of the world that is right and—because it is right—people follow it. Part of the rightness is about the people, and part of it is about the ideas.

What I do is look and say, "Is there something people are not realizing that if they understood it, it would help them think differently and more effectively about the future?" I am trying to draw a map of the future based on observations about reality.

Your approach to leading ideas and starting movements doesn't seem to involve a lot of ego or being concerned with how much recognition you personally are getting out of it. Is that intentional?

I care about people getting the right ideas, and I always have. I want something to happen in the world. But it's not about what I want. We have this line at O'Reilly: "Create more value than you capture."

I was in a brainstorm about the future of the US economy recently, and it was all about the decline of the middle class. It reminded me of so many conversations that I have had with publishers. They ask, "How are we going to preserve our place in the ecosystem?" And I say, "Nobody cares about that. That's the wrong question." The right question is, "What does the world need? What do my customers need? What can I do?"

In the case of the economy, I don't want to hear if we need to preserve the American middle class. That is going to be a by-product of something we do. We should be asking, "What are the big problems in America that we should be tackling?"

So you have to clarify: Who is your actual target? What are you actually trying to accomplish in the world? Everything else should flow from that. That's what I mean by putting things in the right order.

Many companies do this wrong, and I have even in my own company. You think, "We need X, Y, Z for us and therefore we will do A, B, C to get it." But all of our more successful projects have been when we have forgotten that. When we were just so excited about changing the world that we went for it.

TIM O'REILLY is the founder and CEO of O'Reilly Media, Inc. He publishes books, runs conferences, invests in early-stage start-ups, urges companies to create more value than they capture, and tries to change the world by spreading and amplifying the knowledge of innovators.

→ www.oreilly.com

"It always seems impossible until it's done."

SOLVING A REAL PROBLEM

—

Emily Heyward

In a perfect world, new ideas would only be generated in response to glaring problems. Yet, as a culture, we've become so obsessed with "innovation"
that we imbue it with an intrinsic value all its own.
We act as if a new idea is good just because it's
new. But what if we were forced to stop and ask
ourselves: *"Why* do we need that?"

From the outside, conjuring up a new idea and launching a business
looks very tempting. Be your own boss, wear a hoodie every day, create a cool app, get bought for a billion. Start-ups and entrepreneurship
are all the rage. But the reality is less glamorous. Most entrepreneurs

have cast off comfortable jobs to embark on years of late nights, doubt, debt, and the constant threat of failure. It takes an almost insane amount of drive to get through those years, to keep going against all odds and at the sacrifice of friends, family, and fitness. (Yes, there is such thing as the "start-up fifteen.") That's why the best entrepreneurs, the most successful ones, are those who saw something that was broken and had no choice but to fix it. They developed their ideas because they saw a problem that desperately needed solving. And that problem wasn't, "I hate my finance job."

DON'T JUST INVENT SOMETHING, FIX SOMETHING

Ideally, the impulse to invent emerges organically, from witnessing—or, even better, experiencing—something that isn't working and then not being able to rest until you fix it. Now, I'm not trying to make the case that every new idea needs to address world hunger (although, wouldn't that be nice?); problems come in all sizes and degrees of weightiness. Maybe the problem is that you can't find a flattering bathing suit, or that your cable bill is frustratingly high. As long as it's real, and it affects people, it's a starting place for meaningful innovation.

Of course, in reality, new ideas don't always come about in direct response to an issue. If you have a creative mind, you might wake up in the middle of the night wondering, "Wouldn't it be cool if . . . ?" Or, you might even deliberately sit down one day and think, "I'm sick of my job. I'm sick of this life. What can I build?" But even if your idea didn't result from a burning desire to fix something—especially if it didn't—you should run it through a rigorous test to ensure it's something the world really needs. And that process starts by asking, "What problem am I solving?"

Whenever I sit down with a new client, one of the very first questions I ask is what issue they are addressing for their users. This may seem like an easy question, but it's surprisingly hard to answer. Without fail, each entrepreneur jumps to the benefits of his or her product instead of the needs of their audience. For instance, someone launching a new gym concept might say, "Getting consistent quality training at an affordable price." Or someone launching a platform for small business owners might respond, "Giving users visibility and ownership of their data." Notice that these are not problems; they are solutions.

Of course, it's natural for entrepreneurs to jump directly to their ideas, which they spend all their time thinking about and obsessing over in the early stages of building their businesses. Presumably they identified the problem long ago and have moved on. But in the early stages of building a brand, the problem you're solving should be a constant guiding light.

Staying focused on the problem also prevents you from falling into the fatal trap of assuming the world is waiting with bated breath for your product to launch. When I used to work in advertising, we would joke that the "insight" in the creative brief was often something along the lines of, "I wish there were a crunchy cereal with raisins that was healthy and also delicious." But people do not wish this. They might have a hard time finding a quick breakfast that doesn't make them feel fat or sluggish. And maybe your crunchy raisin cereal is the perfect response to this issue. But they are not waking up in the morning wishing for raisiny, crunchy goodness. Similarly, people are not wishing for your idea to exist, because they don't even know it's an option. So when you sit down to clarify what problem you're solving, a great initial test is to imagine someone's inner monologue. Is the problem you've identified something that a real human might actually be thinking?

FIREPROOFING YOUR IDEA WITH THE "WHY?" TEST

Once you've identified the problem—a desire or need that a real person might actually have—then it's time to go deeper. This is called the "why test." Have you ever spent time with a two-year-old that keeps asking "Why?" no matter what response you give? It's time to channel that two-year-old. Let's travel back in time and imagine ourselves in the nineteenth-century equivalent of a hoodie, perhaps it's a mid-length sack coat, which, according to *Wikipedia*, replaced the frock coat for less formal occasions. And, exciting news, we just invented the car! Pretty amazing, right? Let's take a moment to congratulate ourselves and imagine the IPO.

So now we have this incredible innovation on our hands, and it's time to figure out what problem we're actually solving. It's not, "People need a personal motorized way to get from point A to point B." Everyone knows the famous Henry Ford quote, "If I had asked people what they wanted, they would have said faster horses." People weren't walking (or riding) around, wishing for a car. But maybe the problem was, "My horse is very slow and he tires easily." OK, why does that matter? "Well, it takes me too long to get places, and I can't travel very far." And why does that matter? "I spend more time getting myself places than enjoying my life and accomplishing things." And why does that matter? "Because I'm going to die pretty soon and I have so much I need to achieve first. I can't waste my short life on the back of this horse!" And we're done. The "why test" always ends with fear of death. That's the only acceptable indication that you've reached the end of the "why" chain, because you could argue that "fear of death" is the ultimate motivator for all human behavior. Only then do you have permission to go back and identify which insight is actually most relevant and appropriate for what you're trying to create.

In the spirit of asking why, you might be asking, "Why does this even matter? We invented the *car*; isn't that enough? Why do we need to keep looking backward and worrying about the problem?" Because this kind of thinking is the difference between launching a product that's just a flash in the pan and building a beloved brand that endures for decades. It ensures that everything you do, from inception through execution, is rooted in the needs of your audience. Instead of simply focusing on what you're building, you are determining why it matters.

It's relatively easy to arrive at a one-sentence description of what your product does. But that's not a brand idea. The best brands, the strongest brands, the ones that everybody loves, stand for a concept that is much greater than the product itself. To use two well-worn examples, Nike isn't about sneakers; it's about performance. Apple isn't about computers; it's about creativity. Perhaps the car stands for freedom. But you won't arrive at that conclusion by starting with your product. You get there by starting with people. What do people need, what do they care about, what are their passions and dreams, their desires and fears? Then, and only then, can you begin to understand how your product fits into the equation.

By focusing on the problem you're solving, you move beyond a functional description of what your product is, to an emotional solution that connects with people at their core. It also keeps us honest that what we're doing really matters, which will perhaps make all those late nights a little easier to bear.

EMILY HEYWARD is a founding partner at Red Antler, a branding consultancy specializing in start-ups and new ventures. She has led branding efforts for companies including Rent the Runway, One Kings Lane, and Vevo.

→ www.redantler.com

"Don't hate, create."

— BEN HOROWITZ

ASKING THE RIGHT QUESTIONS

–

Warren Berger

"One does not begin with answers," the legendary business consultant Peter Drucker once remarked. "One begins by asking, 'What are our questions?'"

The notion that questions may sometimes be more valuable to a business than answers is counterintuitive. But ask some of today's top business leaders and entrepreneurs, and you'll find they share Drucker's assessment of the critical importance of focusing on questions. "Asking the right questions is the number one thing I spend my time thinking about these days," says Dev Patnaik of Jump Associates, a strategy firm that helps companies innovate. Eric Ries, meanwhile, finds that as he trains companies in the Lean Startup methodology, one of his biggest challenges is getting his clients to "acknowledge uncertainty and ask the seemingly dumb questions."

Questioning is perhaps most important when you're at that critical stage of forming a company and developing a clear sense of mission and purpose. The questions you ask will guide the choices you make, the directions you move in, the opportunities you pursue (or fail to pursue), and the culture you create.

The relatively easy questions are the practical ones that are asked on a routine basis: How can we do this or that task a bit more efficiently? Where can we save a few dollars? But questions that address mission and purpose—the "why" of your business— are more challenging. Here are seven such questions. Tackle them early—but learn to live with them, too, because these are questions you should keep asking, again and again, as your business grows and matures.

1. WHY ARE WE HERE IN THE FIRST PLACE?

Most start-ups begin with a clear sense of purpose: someone sets out to solve a problem, meet a need, answer a question that's been driving them crazy. Think about some recent ones like Nest, Square, or Dropbox—they all got into business because they passionately believed there was something lacking or missing in the world (a smart thermostat, a means to enable anyone to accept credit cards, a better way of storing data). That's a tremendous motivator and a great way to start a business—but it's easy to lose sight of that driving purpose as the business becomes a reality. Day-to-day survival issues and financial pressures start to take over. Companies can quickly lose sight of what really matters. So you have to keep that "Why are we here?" question front and center at all times (put a banner on the wall if you must). To quote Dropbox's Drew Houston, when we're focused on the main goal, the thing that really matters, it's like we're "a dog chasing a tennis ball." Don't take your eye off that tennis ball.

2. IF WE DISAPPEARED, WHO WOULD MISS US? AND WHY?

This question was shared with me by Doug Rauch, former president of Trader Joe's. "It's a question every company should ask itself," Rauch says, because it brings into focus what makes you unique and valuable, while also clarifying who your core customers are and why they need you. If you can't answer this question specifically (hint: "everybody" is not a good answer), you need to work on it.

3. WHAT BUSINESS ARE WE REALLY IN?

This question forces you to explore your deeper relationship with customers—beyond just the obvious product or service you're offering. Nike started out selling athletic shoes but figured out early on that its real business was addressing active-lifestyle needs of all kinds. This enabled it to expand its offering and to evolve as its customers' lives evolved. Continually asking this question becomes even more important in times of dynamic change. The business you started out in last month may not even exist next year, but if you've identified the real value you offer to the world, you can adapt and survive even as the market around you changes.

4. HOW CAN WE BECOME A CAUSE AND NOT JUST A COMPANY?

Sure you've got a great product; so do lots of people. If you want to really form a bond with customers, ask yourself how you can connect with them on a deeper level—one that taps into something people really care about. Today, discriminating consumers and talented employees are drawn to brands and companies that stand for something worthwhile. But the stand you take must be authentic and appropriate. Ask yourself, "What does the world need ... that we are uniquely able to provide?" Panera's CEO Ron Shaich tackled that question and it led to the launch of Panera Cares, an initiative to open a number of pay-what-you-can cafés that are identical to the chain's other restaurants, except customers pay what they wish or can afford. Panera had bread; the world was hungry. Panera connected these two realities in a way that turned the company into a cause.

5. WHAT ARE WE WILLING TO SACRIFICE?

Shaich told me that as the company was developing the Panera Cares idea and putting it into practice (with the CEO himself working on location at the first café), some tough choices had to be made in order to ensure the integrity of the program: offering a full menu instead of a limited one, and so forth. At each step, Shaich says, the company had to ask: Do we want to take a shortcut on this, or do it right? Being true to a mission or cause often requires making tough decisions. "When you come to the point where you can't serve both the bottom line and the cause, one or the other must suffer," says consultant Tim Ogilvie of Peer Insight. He points to the example of Whole Foods being willing to stop selling live lobsters for an extended period of time until it could find a supplier that did humane harvesting. "Those are hard choices, but when you opt for the cause over the bottom line, people can see that," Ogilvie says. "And then they believe in the company and the cause even more."

6. HOW CAN WE MAKE A BETTER EXPERIMENT?

According to Lean Startup's Eric Ries, this is a critical question—though most businesses never think to ask it. The primary concern is usually with 'making products,' not 'making experiments.' But the way to make better products is by first getting better at experimentation. Ries says you start with the acknowledgment that "we are operating amid uncertainty—and that the purpose of building a product or doing any other activity is to create an experiment to reduce that uncertainty." This means that instead of asking the question, 'What will we make?,' the emphasis should be on 'What will we learn?' "And then you work backwards to the simplest possible thing—the minimum viable product—that can get you the learning," he says. A side benefit is that this approach can help unlock the creativity that's already there in your company. "Most companies are full of ideas, but they don't know how to go about finding out if those ideas work," Ries says. "If you want to harvest all those ideas, allow employees to experiment more—so they can find out the answers to their questions themselves."

7. WHAT IS OUR MISSION QUESTION?

This is not to be confused with your mission statement—you know, that thing you write down that gets stashed away in a drawer somewhere.

Your mission statement is probably more of an ad slogan than an accurate depiction of your ideals. But that's another discussion; what I'm talking about here is a forward-looking, open-ended goal that is best expressed as an unanswered question. Right now we offer a pretty good X, but how might we go beyond that and offer X, Y, and Z? How might we take what we do and use it to actually change the world? You don't have to answer the question anytime soon; it may take years to get there. So make it bold and ambitious. Give yourself something to pursue. Share it with all your partners, from the people who work for you to your customers. It tells them that you are on a journey that matters. It acknowledges room for possibility, change, and adaptability. It challenges you—and it invites others to help you answer this question.

Keep asking yourself these seven questions—and lots of other ones—and it will help you figure out what you're doing, why you're doing it, and how you might do it better. As Panera's Shaich says: "Figuring out what you want to accomplish is a continual search—and questions are the means to the search."

WARREN BERGER *is the author of* A More Beautiful Question: The Power of Inquiry to Spark Breakthrough Ideas.

→ www.amorebeautifulquestion.com

KEY
TAKEAWAYS

—

Defining Your Purpose

Get more insights and the desktop wallpaper at:

→ www.99u.com/purpose

· PURPOSE IS YOUR COMPASS

Do the hard work of uncovering your purpose and summarizing it succinctly. It brings into focus the things that matter most, and provides a roadmap for future actions.

· FIND YOUR "WHY"

Use the "why" test to drill down to the real problem your product will solve, and lay the groundwork for a brand that people can connect with deeply.

· UPGRADE YOUR OPERATING SYSTEM

Complement your vision with a dedication to lean business practices, open collaboration, and an emphasis on learning and experimenting.

· LOOK OUTWARD, NOT INWARD

Don't focus on what you need, focus on what the world needs. Follow your enthusiasm, your intuition, and your customers.

· BE A GIVER, NOT A TAKER

Every time you make a decision, look at how your business can "create more value than it captures," as they say at O'Reilly Media.

· ASK HARD QUESTIONS, ALL THE TIME

View your business itself as a product that you are constantly iterating on, tinkering with, and evolving. There are no answers without questions.

CHAPTER TWO

BUILDING YOUR PRODUCT

–

How to design, test, launch, and refine an incredible product experience

Product is a clinical term for a passionate endeavor. As Steve Jobs, the "product guy" par excellence, put it: "Every good product I've ever seen is because a group of people cared deeply about making something wonderful that they and their friends wanted. They wanted to use it themselves."

Captured in that statement are the twin ideals that guide all great product development: an unstoppable enthusiasm for bringing something great into the world and a relentless focus on usability.

Your mission, should you choose to accept it, is to develop a laserlike focus on making one thing great. To dedicate yourself to relentless iteration and prototyping, so that you can fail fast and learn fast. To privilege your user above all and create an experience that's simple, effortless, and delightful.

But remember: The proof is in the process. Crafting a killer product takes time, so make sure you figure out how to have fun while you're doing it.

GETTING ONE THING RIGHT

—

Andy Dunn

Consumers don't need many things from your brand—they just need one thing from your brand. You may want them to need everything from you, but guess what: consumers don't care what you want. Your job is to care about what they want, not what you want them to want. The difference between the two is the distance between a customer-centric company and an egocentric company.

A lot of brands don't make it because in the process of trying to get many things right, they don't get anything right. A great brand is a privilege, and it's a privilege best earned through an item, not through a collection. Designers and merchants and founders think about collections. Consumers think about items.

That's why the best way to start is by getting one thing right. That earns you the right to go from product one to product two. Take as much time as you need to get product one right, and to prove it— because if you don't, no one is going to be waiting on pins and needles for product two.

The stories about the singular products that launched great brands crowd out the stories about the singular brands that started with many great products. You know where I'm going: Ralph Lauren and a tie, Diane von Furstenberg and a wrap dress, Potbelly and a heated sandwich, Theory and a women's pant, Tory Burch and a ballet flat, Kate Spade and a handbag, Google and a single search box on a clean page, Warby Parker and a pair of glasses.

You want your inaugural product to be wanted badly by your inaugural users, and that is hard to do with multiple products. Y Combinator co-founder Paul Graham has written expertly on this in his seminal essay "How to Get Startup Ideas":

> *When a start-up launches, there have to be at least some users who really need what it's making—not just people who could see themselves using it one day, but who want it urgently. Usually this initial group of users is small, for the simple reason that if there were something that large numbers of people urgently needed and that could be built with the amount of*

The moral is this: if you don't start with a relentless focus on an amazing first product, odds are you won't even get a seat at the table. You don't start with the right to do product #2. You earn it.

At Bonobos, it has taken years to perfect our first product: men's pants—and we're still doing work every day to make them better. My co-founder, Brian Spaly, began developing the idea for better pants in 2005 when we were roommates at Stanford business school. He conducted lean consumer research in 2006 on our classmates, including me. He wanted to know what kinds of pants we wore, what we thought about them, and where we bought them.

What he discovered is no one really liked their pants. He developed the first prototypes, "Spaly-pants," to solve this problem in 2007. The Spaly-pants really did fit better—with an innovative contoured waistband and a tailored fit through the seat and thigh that threaded the needle on the "American pants are too boxy, European pants are too tight" conundrum. He made them in pliable fabrics, some in bright colors, and all with eye-catching contrast pocket liners that emphasized the attention to detail and joy put into the product. You know you have a hit product when you have $10,000 in cash in your hands from your first production run, which Brian soon did.

When I realized Brian's hobby could become a company, I began helping him. Eventually, at his invitation, I became the founding CEO. We teamed up and sold pants like crazy for the next six months to everyone we knew. We did trunk shows. We did pants parties. I took a duffel bag of pants everywhere I went, including to weddings in LA and Hawaii, where I still get grief for being the guy hawking pants at brunch or over poolside mai tais.

We didn't begin angel investor conversations until we had tens of thousands of dollars of sales; until we knew "the dogs were eating the dog food," as our founding angel investor, Andy Rachleff, likes to say. This is the opposite of the model where you raise seed money before you know if your product even works. We were lucky to be able to do this because Brian had saved money to invest in the working capital to start the company, and I cashed in a 401(k) to be salary-free as our CEO for the first several months.

We never thought about a second product. In fact, I had one slide in the appendix of our initial angel investor deck that showed the progression of products we might make years down the road in the event that we were successful, and I'll never forget what Andy Rachleff told me: "I don't want you even thinking about this stuff until you have proven you can sell pants."

We captured sales in an Excel file, and we collected money the old-school way: cash and checks. Ninety percent of customers who tried on the pants purchased. Twenty-five percent of customers purchased three or more pairs. We sold 475 pairs of pants that summer. We hadn't even launched e-commerce yet, but we had $50,000 in trailing revenue from selling in person and through the mail.

We were now ready for a more scalable selling model, e-commerce. That summer, I recruited another Stanford classmate, Erik Allebest, who had built the largest chess e-commerce site in the US, to become our e-commerce advisor. Prior to my move to NYC, we spent the summer of 2007 in a yurt behind his house in Menlo Park building what would become the first version of Bonobos e-commerce: a now defunct site called www.bonobospants.com.

When we launched the site in October of 2007, we redoubled our in-person selling efforts. We sold more, not less, to feed our new automated selling engine with demand. We expanded our trunk shows to Chicago, Philadelphia, DC, and Boston. We also began to get great editorial PR without asking for it. Men's e-magazine *Urban-Daddy* ran a story on us, and it drove so much traffic that it crashed our site. That was also our first $2,000 day.

With great PR, word of mouth, continued in-person selling, and some very limited experimentation with online marketing, we hit $1 million in revenue run-rate six months after our e-commerce launch. Six months later that number had doubled to $2 million.

I marvel when I reflect on this. We only had one single pant style, and an exaggerated boot cut at that. We didn't offer inseams yet, so most likely you had to get the pants hemmed. We only had a handful of fabric choices, in about a dozen colors—a small fraction of what we now offer. We didn't have denim yet, and we didn't have khaki chinos. And there was no way to try the pants on before you bought them.

Yet we saw a hockey stick–style growth ramp. How could this be?

We hit a nerve with our product. A lot of men's pants don't fit that well. We were 100 percent focused on it, and the fit was better than what most guys were used to. We also hit a nerve with our service model. A lot of men don't like traditional shopping—we offered a new kind of experience: digital at its core and more personal as enabled by our team of customer service ninjas. We were crystal clear about our messaging: come to us because you want great pants, and you want a better way to get them.

Six years on, the original boot-cut style we launched with now comprises less than 10 percent of our pants business. Pants are now less than 40 percent of our total business. And we have brick-and-mortar "Guideshops" in several cities nationwide, where you can try our pants on for size, get expert style advice, and have your purchase shipped to your doorstep. We've come a long way, but we would never have made it here if it weren't for that first product.

<hr>

Here's the paradox: even if you make two great items right out of the gates, just by having two you make it harder for the customer to know what job to hire you for. Why start with two, when it creates more risk, requires more capital, dilutes your focus, and makes it harder to message who you are in those precious early innings? Remember: you'll have opportunities to grow revenue and extend the brand later.

Our CFO loves to remind me: "Money runs out faster than opportunities."

ANDY DUNN is an entrepreneur focused on building great consumer Internet companies. He is the CEO and founder of Bonobos, Inc., the parent company of Bonobos, Maide golf, and AYR, as well as the founder of angel investment firm Red Swan Ventures.

→ www.bonobos.com

"It is only by selection, by elimination, and by emphasis that we get at the real meaning of things."

— GEORGIA O'KEEFFE

MAKING EXPERIENCES, NOT PRODUCTS

—

Scott Belsky

There's a lot of talk lately about "making product," as if the process is one-sided—under complete control of the maker. Sure, design and engineering are central to making a great product, but it turns out that great product creators aren't just makers; they are also stewards.

For your customer, the product is ultimately his or her experience of it and nothing more. So when you are creating and evolving a product, your primary role is really managing the experience of those who will use it. Which means that, at the end of the day, a great product maker must have empathy for the user's experience.

Over the years, I have been involved with developing many products: some physical ones, like a line of "Action" organizational notebooks; some digital, like Behance as well as start-ups I have advised like Pinterest and Uber; some offline experiences, like the 99U Conference and my book *Making Ideas Happen*, as well as collaborating with Jocelyn on this book series. Along the way, I have developed my own approach to product stewardship and have observed best practices from those that I have worked with.

GROUND YOUR AMBITION AND MAINTAIN SIMPLICITY

Be wary of the creator's tendency to add more and more features and options. Grand visions must be boiled down to be effective visions. While the intricacies of your product may fascinate you, it's quite possible that they complicate the product and frustrate your users. All too often, great products gain an edge through their simplicity in the beginning (which is usually a matter of expediency), only to become overly complex or bloated as they are evolved. I call it the "Cycle of Simplicity Loss," and it plays out like this:

- *Step 1: Users flock to simple product.*

- *Step 2: Simple product adds features and evolves, taking users for granted.*

- *Step 3: Users flock to a different—more simple—product.*

Most software falls victim to this cycle. A program like Microsoft Word or Outlook starts as a simple processor or mail program, adds a ton of features, and then creates a need for Google Docs or Gmail. The trick here is to stay sober about your product by regularly boiling down every aspect of it for the first-time user. Doing so brings you back to the roots of why your product is important and what made it effective in the first place.

HELP YOUR CUSTOMERS SURVIVE THE FIRST FIFTEEN SECONDS

Everyone you meet—and everyone that visits your website or uses your products—must first be convinced that they should care about your product. Why? Because we are all lazy in the first fifteen seconds of any new experience. This is not intended as a cynical jibe at humanity. I believe it's an essential insight for building great products and experiences both online and off.

We are lazy in the sense that we don't want to invest much time or energy in truly understanding what something is. We are impatient and distracted. Life has such a steep learning curve as it is, with seldom enough time for work, play, learning, and love. And so, when something entirely new requires too much effort, we just let it pass. Overly complicated sell pages, laborious unpacking, extensive sign-up processes, and other friction points that obstruct getting an immediate return from engagement are alienating. New customers need something quick now, regardless of what they may get later.

The greatest product design teams I know take this laziness to heart and use it to ground their development process. Just one example: at Behance, in the very first version of the sign-up process for our service, we asked new members to select their top three creative fields. New users took an average of 120 seconds to browse the list and select their top fields. We lost around 10 percent of new members during this particular part of the sign-up process. So we ultimately decided to remove it from the sign-up process and capture the information later, once the user was active on the website. The result? Sign-ups skyrocketed.

For better or worse, meaningful engagement—with products and services (especially the Internet kind)—occurs only when we're pulled past the initial laziness and selfishness that accompanies any new experience.

But what pulls us through? The hook.

BE SURE TO HAVE A HOOK

An effective hook appeals to short-term interests (aka our selfishness and impatience) but is connected to a long-term promise. When you see a prompt to "Sign Up in Seconds to Organize Your Life," it's a hook. The headlines we read in newspapers are hooks. Dating sites are full of hooks.

Let's take the process of purchasing a book as an example. Regardless of how well written and interesting it may be, the book is nothing but hundreds of pages of black-and-white words (or a digital file) until you actually commit to reading it. The hook, in this case, is the cover. The cover paints a pretty picture that hopefully sparks your curiosity and compels you to pick it up.

Without a hook—be it a slick package, a great tagline, or a killer thirty-second pitch video—you're unlikely to capture the user's attention. And if you can't do that, the deeper experience doesn't matter, because they're never going to get there.

The challenge is to create product experiences for two different mind-sets. In retail, what you display in your windows determines whether or not a customer will walk in. But the science of window dressing is entirely different from in-store merchandising and the actual quality of your products. In publishing, the cover of your book will determine whether or not people will pick it up, but the art of cover design is entirely different from the art of great writing. When you try to create both the cover and the book—or the window dressing and the product selection—with the same goals in mind, you're liable to fail at both.

As you build your product or service, take a two-track approach. Optimize the product experience for the first fifteen seconds as a compartmentalized project. Then, for the customers that actually come through the door, build a meaningful experience and a relationship that lasts a lifetime. In other words, make decisions with the short-term as well as the long-term in mind.

THE DEVIL IS IN THE DEFAULT

Another insight on product stewardship that I've learned is that users don't follow directions. For instance, when was the last time you read an instruction manual? Most people don't. Instead, they just dive in and start exploring.

People will quickly become acquainted with your product and discover the surface features without your assistance. The vast majority of your users will continue to use the product with just those initial features that they discovered at the outset. Have you ever used the "Return to Last Channel Watched" button on your remote control? Have you ever used your iPhone to set reminders based on your location? Have you programmed your computer to use the keyboard shortcuts that let you type a few letters to insert commonly used sentences? None of these features are part of the default user experience, and so you likely do not use them.

Dave Morin, co-founder and CEO of the mobile social network Path, likes to say that "the devil is in the default." While you may have a lot of other things to offer, the "default experience"—the one that happens without any additional learning or customization from the user—will determine the success or failure of your product. Which means that the default experience is the one you want to focus on the most. It's difficult to do this because you, as the product's creator, will always be an advanced user. But your newest users will always matter more than you.

Never forget that creating a product is creating an experience. Your job is not only to give your customers something valuable but to help them use it.

You are the steward of your user's experience. Proceed accordingly.

SCOTT BELSKY is Adobe's vice president of product/ community and co-founder of Behance, the leading online platform for creatives to showcase and discover creative work. Scott has been called one of the "100 Most Creative People in Business" by Fast Company, and is the author of the international bestseller Making Ideas Happen. He is also an investor and advisor for several companies, including Pinterest and Uber.

→ www.scottbelsky.com

"Excellence is doing ordinary things extraordinarily well."

— E. F. SCHUMACHER

Q&A:

ITERATING YOUR WAY TO INNOVATION

—

with Sebastian Thrun

Sebastian Thrun knows how to create big, bold products that change the world. He led the team that created Google Glass and the Google Self-Driving Car, and is the co-founder of Udacity, which is tackling the new frontier of how to democratize education by delivering a great learning experience online. All of these creations started out as complex, knotty problems with solutions that seemed nearly unimaginable. And yet, little by little, Thrun shepherded his teams to an answer. We talked with him about the importance of iterating relentlessly, and what to do when fear and doubt tempt you to waiver from your course.

You've developed a number of revolutionary products. How do you focus your energies at the beginning of a project?

When thinking about products, I like to use a mountain-climbing analogy. The first step is to pick a peak. Don't pick a peak because it's easy. Pick a peak because you really want to go there; that way you'll enjoy the process.

The second thing is to pick a team you trust and that's willing to learn with you. Because the way mountain climbing really works is that you can't climb the entire route perfectly. You have to know that you are going to make mistakes, that you'll have to turn around, and that you'll have to recover.

You also have to maintain your sense of purpose. For a long time, it may feel like you're on the wrong path, but you must have the resilience to forge ahead. You just have to keep moving uphill.

It sounds like it's more about focusing on the process for you, as opposed to the outcome.

Absolutely. For me, the journey is much more delightful if you can derive pleasure from the process every day, rather than at the end of the year. If your goal is to IPO and get rich, then you're going to be in for a very long, very sad ride. Because most people don't IPO and don't get rich.

Our most important asset is our time, so I think it's best to manage your time well right now and be happy about it, rather than focus on some deferred goal, like buying a fancy car in the future. The data shows that people who are rich aren't any happier, so you might as well derive your happiness from what you are doing today.

How does iteration figure into your process? Do you think it's best to create a functional prototype as soon as possible?

To return to the mountain idea, if you think about it, there's no other way to get up the mountain than taking a hundred thousand steps. You could have all the meetings and all the documentation and work for weeks on end to make the perfect plan. But in my opinion, all you've done at that point is lost time. You've done nothing. You've learned nothing.

Sure, if this mountain has been climbed ten thousand times before, then you just get the book, and the maps, and you follow the same steps. But that's not innovation. Innovation is about climbing a mountain that no one has climbed before. So there ought to be some unknowns along the way because no one has solved the problem yet.

And when you're innovating, sheer thinking just won't work. What gets you there is fast iteration, and fast failing. And when you fail, you've done something great: you've learned something. In hindsight, it might look a little embarrassing, and people will say, "You should've known that." But the truth is you couldn't have known because it's unchartered territory. Almost every entrepreneur I know has failed massively many, many times along the way.

What's the most common mistake that people make when they're developing a product?

One mistake I see a lot is the eternal thinker, the perfectionist. This is the person that builds all the components without putting them together, because there's perfection in component development. And they have this idea that if you only put things together right before launch, everything will go fine. Of course, that never happens.

The second mistake I see is more of a character issue, which is being discouraged by failure. Where you do something three or four times, spend half a year in development, and think, "Oh my god, I'm not there yet, let me change my career . . ." So that's a lack of perseverance.

The last one I see is being driven by fear. When your competitor does something new, you become fearful and decide that you're going to change course. But every single time you do this, you're already behind your competitor and that's just a bad idea. You have to have faith in yourself, and believe in your vision.

At some time, everybody is driven by fear. But we need to—as much as we can—take fear out of the game. One way to do this is to imagine that you are already successful. You've looked into the future, and you've succeeded. What would you enjoy doing today given that knowledge?

Clearly, certain personality types are more comfortable with iteration and failure than

others. Do you think you can learn to be if it doesn't come naturally?

It's obvious to me that there's a certain personality type that can deal with failure more than others. But I think this awareness can also be acquired, especially when you realize that the failures that come out of experimentation really don't relate to you as a person. It's just the course of innovation; failure is a systemic part of that process.

For instance, if you're driving a car, and after three hundred miles the car runs out of gas, no one takes offense because the "failure" is inherent to the car, not to you. It's not your failure to operate the car correctly. We all know that you have to refill the gas tank; that's just the way it is. So if we think of failure in innovation in the same way—as having to refill the gas tank regularly—we can take it much less personally.

That's a great metaphor. So you think the idea of constant—and playful—experimentation is the best mind-set for innovation?

It's very uncommon for people to have the attitude of "Wow, I don't know." In childhood, researchers call this a "growth mind-set"—this idea that you're comfortable with the fact that you just don't know something yet, or that you just can't do something yet. But most people are raised with this feeling that they know everything.

But if you know everything, you can't possibly innovate, right? It's impossible, because there is nothing new to learn or discover.

There's this funny saying that I like: "After high school, kids know everything, after their bachelor's degree, they know something, and after a PhD, they now know that they know nothing."

I think that the ability to see how much more there is to know and be humble about it is actually a good thing. Returning to the mountain metaphor, every mountain climber I know of feels small in the mountains and enjoys the feeling of being small. No matter what you do, the mountain is always bigger than you are.

SEBASTIAN THRUN *is CEO of Udacity, a start-up focused on democratizing higher education. He is also a part-time Google fellow and research professor at Stanford University.*

→ www.udacity.com

"Life shrinks or expands in proportion to one's courage."

— ANAÏS NIN

TREATING YOUR USERS
LIKE COLLABORATORS

—

Jane ni Dhulchaointigh

The absolute privilege of our time is that we can hear our users talking—and like never before, we can listen. So listen. While we pride ourselves on our creativity at my company, Sugru, almost every product decision we've made originated in the incredibly fertile ground of our user submissions and things we've heard our users say. We've changed our packaging, changed our website, changed the colors we offer, changed our product line . . . The list goes on.

Whether you embrace it or not, you are not the only one who is building your product or business—your users are, too. And by involving your users at every turn—before, during, and after launch—you can not only reap untold advantages as a business; you'll also have the most amazing time along the way.

But let me start at the beginning . . . At twenty-three, I moved to London with high hopes of becoming a brilliant product designer. No more sculpture for me. I loved stuff, and I wanted to channel my creativity to improve everyday life for myself and others. This was a genius career move. It was going to be perfect!

Well, not quite. It only took a few weeks at the Royal College of Art to see that this design lark was much more complex than I'd thought. Two realizations began to dawn: (a) I wasn't very good at it, and (b) all this new stuff we were supposed to design—did anyone really need it? Isn't there enough stuff in the world?

Lost and struggling to find a foothold, I hid myself away in the workshop and tried to find some thinking space. I think with my hands, so I started making. Instead of designing products, maybe I could explore the materials they were made of. I broke down things like wood, foam, and concrete and put them back together in different combinations. One day, I mixed together silicone with waste wood dust. This new material looked like wood, but I could shape it in my hands. I formed it into a ball and left it on a workbench.

After lunch, it felt hard. Something made me throw it on the ground. What happened next made me break out into laughter and run into the studio next door to find someone to show. When the ball landed on the ground, it didn't just bounce a little; it bounced a lot! Right back up into the room like a ping-pong ball. This moment of delight caused me to begin an obsessive search to find the purpose of this odd stuff I'd made. For weeks I searched high and low for the one big problem or opportunity it might solve, until I ran out of steam.

It was at the point of giving up that I found the material's purpose, right there, under my nose. I'd used leftovers of the mixture around the house to fix my kitchen sink plug and change the shape of an uncomfortable knife handle. Comforting my tears of frustration, my boyfriend, James, helped me see what I'd done and what it could mean.

The penny dropped. What if this material could turn anyone into a designer? What if everyone could improve, adapt, and fix things so they worked better for longer? A whole new world opened up in my mind where we didn't need to keep buying new stuff all the time. We have enough stuff—we just need to make it work better! The idea for Sugru was born. I'm not a scientist, but my idea—creating a unique form of self-setting rubber that could rival Super Glue or Scotch tape in its utility and popularity—required some pretty heavyweight R&D, and I was on a mission to make it happen. Pretty soon, I met and teamed up with my co-founder, Roger Ashby, who was able to introduce me to some top scientists from the silicone industry as well as intellectual property experts to protect our work.

Initially, I thought we'd develop Sugru by working with contract laboratories—hiring experts to do the job. But after I spent £5,000 in three weeks for three experiments and learned nothing, I knew the only way to make this happen was to do it myself. I spent the next £5,000 setting up a laboratory, and the next three years mixing small sample batches and painstakingly observing their performance while we edged closer and closer to the physical properties and material behaviors required. It was a long slog, and the thing that got me through it was the user trials I ran on the side while we continued to prototype.

I liked telling people I met about my work. I could see that some folks didn't quite get it, but there were others whose faces lit up. "That sounds incredible! Can I try some?" they would say. I added people to my e-mail list, and as I started to get better results from my laboratory work, I would mail out little parcels of samples for them to demo. By the time we launched, this group of guinea pigs comprised about 150 people from all walks of life—carpenters, chefs, surfers, and others using Sugru to make little fixes around the home. Almost all of them would send me pictures and feedback about how they'd used the product, and I pinned them up on the large bulletin boards that grew to cover the wall of our little office.

This process functioned like time travel for me. I thought of these people as if they were from the future, and I was able to touch and feel what it would be like to have Sugru out in the world, with real people using it. It's a trick of the imagination, but the tangible evidence kept me going through the toughest of times.

I also ended up learning a ton about the value of actively engaging and listening to your users. Incredible things happen if you keep your eye on the prize and your ear to the ground. Here are a few observations about how to do it.

1. Put your product in the user's hands before it's perfect. See what happens.

Right from the very start, I put my early prototype material in people's hands. When I gave it to a family and asked them to find uses for it, I saw that they treated it like modeling clay and made what they would have made with clay. Right then, I learned in less than an hour that to achieve my mission of helping people to hack, modify, and improve existing products with Sugru, the communications around the material would be just as important—maybe even more so!—than the material itself. I didn't learn this by asking questions of my trial users. Someone clever once said, "Ask a dumb question, you'll get a dumb answer." I learned it by setting up a situation, observing, and reflecting.

2. Show your users what they *can* do, rather than telling them what they *should* do.

Early on in the development process, I made a small book of illustrations—one hundred uses for this magical material called Sugru—some were practical, but most were daft or funny. People smiled and laughed, and the most common questions were "Where can I get it?" and "How much is it?"

The product was still in the nascent development stage, and I had to say, "I'll let you know as soon as it's available!" and took down their e-mail addresses. I didn't know then just how long it would take me to arrive at a final product—six years!—or that when I would finally get there, those illustrations would still be as fresh as they were the day I drew them. But when we launched our website years later, they featured prominently and had pretty much the same effect of making people smile and imagine the possibilities.

The point is, we could tell people that Sugru was for fixing, modifying, and improving stuff as much as we wanted, but if we didn't show them the possibilities, they probably wouldn't get it. Telling someone that they could customize the grip on their cutting sheers or adapt their earbuds to fit their ears properly proved much less powerful than simply showing them snapshots of everyday objects hacked with Sugru. Especially when it comes to a creative customer base, visuals can make those "aha!" lightbulbs go off instantly.

3. Empower your users to be your ambassadors, their word is more powerful than yours.

The two things all these trial users had in common was that they believed in our mission—that more people should be able to fix and improve things—and they were enthusiastic about the product. In short, they were like us. So we built our brand to get them excited and to get ourselves excited. We put our mission front and center, and once we had momentum, we shifted from showcasing my early illustrations to showcasing what our users were doing with the product. Rather than show what we did with Sugru (why should you believe us?), we wanted to show what this small community of people were doing with Sugru—believe them!

Since then, Sugru has grown almost entirely by word of mouth. Of course, this couldn't have happened if the product didn't work brilliantly, but the key thing that has enabled it is the culture of people sharing their fixes in order to inspire others to do the same. Our website and social channels are full of real people demonstrating their fixes and projects every day. This culture of sharing didn't just happen by itself, however. We nurtured it by designing for people who were likely to share their insights (e.g., people who love learning, sharing, and spending time online), and by connecting on a personal level with all our early users.

—∞—

As we scale, we continue to try to connect as personally as possible with everyone who shares their experiences with us. Their time, enthusiasm, and generosity need to be acknowledged and rewarded. We champion not only the most useful uses of Sugru but the most "Sugru" behaviors. We give prizes sometimes, but the most effective reward we've found is the most fundamental: as a community, we are collaborating toward a common goal, and that in itself, when it is recognized and reinforced through genuine conversation, is the most powerful reward.

JANE NI DHULCHAOINTIGH is the Irish inventor and CEO of Sugru, a self-setting rubber for fixing, modifying, and improving your stuff. Sugru was named alongside the iPad by TIME magazine as one of "The 50 Best Inventions of 2010."

→ www.sugru.com

"Good design is as little design as possible."

— DIETER RAMS

DESIGNING YOUR PRODUCT TO WORK, LIKE MAGIC

—

Julie Zhuo

The word "design" has traditionally been used to describe the happy marriage of function and form. A chair can be comfortable and beautiful. An invitation can be clear and convey the personality of the event. Every object that serves a functional purpose can be made to not just work but be pleasurable to use and behold, representing the deep craftsmanship that we humans are capable of. But in this day and age, thinking of product design as form—as something purely visual—feels limiting.

We are no longer constrained by what physical objects can afford, so the tasks made possible by the computers, phones, and gadgets in our lives are becoming increasingly complex. I can tell my husband the name of the restaurant we're going to tonight while driving on the other side of town and not interrupt him if he's in a meeting. I can find a French black-and-white coming-of-age movie to watch instantly in the comforts of my living room. I can go to dinner with twelve people and split the bill between us in a way that doesn't involve a messy transfer of bills or forcing the restaurant to swipe twelve separate credit cards. In these examples, what something looks like becomes a smaller and smaller part of what makes the entire experience feel great. More often than not, the questions I ask myself when encountering a new innovation are: 1) Does this make my life better? and 2) Is it easy to use?

Many of the new services or products I appreciate the most tend to have little in the way of new visuals. In fact, they tend to achieve better ease of use by shifting toward invisible design—cutting out entire steps, ditching whole surface areas, or relying on existing patterns instead of inventing new ones. The result is experiences that feel seamless and intuitive, almost magical.

Consider the Internet directories and portals from the early 1990s—Yahoo, Lycos, AOL, and the like. When Yahoo first began in 1994, it was called "Jerry's guide to the World Wide Web." Even when the name changed to Yahoo, the original acronym stood for "Yet Another Hierarchical Officious Oracle." In the infancy of the web, when the number of websites was manageable, it made sense to group them into hierarchical buckets that you could dive into and explore further: Arts and Humanities, Reference, Science, Government. Back then, the most successful businesses were the ones that did the best job of collecting and organizing the content across the Internet.

As the number of websites doubled, quadrupled, and grew exponentially, however, the question arose of how to go about improving these directories in the face of such massive scale. If you were solely focused on what was visible, you might be inclined to revamp the navigation of these directories—maybe add drop-down menus under each top-level category to help the user better narrow her focus while browsing. Or you might launch a series of new portal sites, each with well-curated content around a particular theme, to highlight for users the top destinations across the Internet.

But we all know how this story unfolds. A faster horse has nothing against the speed and comfort of a car, and so it was for improving directories. Ultimately, a single rectangular text field backed by a sophisticated algorithm proved to be a much better design than scores and scores of beautiful portal pages. The era of browsing was over; the era of search had begun.

A more recent example is the growing popularity of services like Dropbox and Box for syncing files across devices or with a group of people. Though there existed many options prior—uploading files via FTP, e-mailing them to yourself, using a version control system, transferring files through external drives, uploading and downloading via file-sharing sites designed to combat this very problem—Dropbox made syncing instantly understandable and seamless to use by adopting the same pattern that many people were already used to when dealing with their digital documents—that of native folders within the operating system. There were no new interfaces to learn, no new screens to get through. The familiarity of working within an existing, well-understood metaphor proved far easier to use than any new app could have been, no matter how simple or beautiful.

How, then, should we consider invisible design as we are building and evolving our own products? It boils down to three simple principles:

1. Don't limit the shape of the solution too early. It's common for people to approach building new products with technological constraints or preconceived notions of what the end solution should look like. Doing this hampers true innovation. Saying, "We need an app that . . ." automatically assumes that the best solution is an app, when maybe it isn't. Instead, as Tesla co-founder Elon Musk advises, work from "first principles." Ask yourself what would need to happen for the problem to be resolved if you were free from all constraints. From there, work your way back into more practical solutions.

2. Reduce the number of steps required. Cut out as many stipulations, actions, unnecessary choices, and extraneous options as you can. An action menu with twenty items is harder to use than an action menu with two, because reading, processing, and deciding among twenty options requires your brain to take many more cognitive steps. Similarly, receiving a poorly packaged product in the mail will require you to get up, find a pair of scissors, do the work of dismantling the packaging, and get rid of annoying packing peanuts or Styrofoam, all of which involve more steps than getting a package with an easy-rip mechanism and no extraneous pieces to dispose of.

3. Look for opportunities to lean on familiar patterns or mental models. For instance, if you're designing a gesture system for an app, conforming to the laws of the physical world makes it easier to understand. If flicking upward expands an object, flicking downward should dismiss it, and ideally all similar objects in the app should behave this way. Likewise, if you are designing an editing interface, don't make the user flip between an "edit" mode with a bunch of input boxes and a "published" mode for display. As in the real world, editing should feel as close to direct manipulation as possible so users don't have to perform a translation of these different models in their heads.

―――――∿―――――

Design is expanding beyond what our eyes can see and beyond what our fingers can touch on a flat screen. The future of design is less and less about discrete objects and more and more about continuous experiences. In the same way that a successful restaurant isn't just about the food but also about the décor, the layout, the service, the drinks, the crowd, and more, all blended together to create something memorable, a successful product is not just what it looks like or even what it can do, but what kind of experience it enables. One day soon, using our voices to get things done will be easier than tapping through a screen. One day soon, smart systems will optimize for us having a flawless experience without needing to pull us into every single minor decision.

For all the pieces of our experience that we do see, may they be beautiful to behold and a testament to craft at the highest level. But for all the things we don't see—may they simply work, as if by magic.

JULIE ZHUO leads the design team focused on engagement and core experiences at Facebook, including News Feed, content discovery, and mobile apps. She's been at Facebook since 2006, helping the service grow to more than one billion users. She also writes about design and product development on Medium.

→ www.medium.com/@joulee

KEY TAKEAWAYS

—

Building Your Product

Get more insights and the desktop wallpaper at:

→ www.99u.com/product

· THE PROBLEM CONTAINS THE SOLUTION

Don't limit the shape of the solution too early in the product development process. Remove constraints, focus on the problem, and work from "first principles."

· THINK SMALL

Focus on making *one* great product that a small group of people truly want. Nail that first; then (and only then) think about expanding your offerings.

· FOCUS ON THE FIRST-TIMERS

Hone your product by empathizing with the first-time user. Assume you have fifteen seconds or less to convince them it's worth their time.

· GO EASY ON YOUR USER

Try to use familiar metaphors when designing your product, rather than inventing new ones, so that users can easily understand how it works.

· FAILURE IS INFORMATION

Start experimenting with, and releasing, prototypes (or beta versions) as soon as possible. If you're not iterating and failing, you're not learning.

· WATCH IT IN THE WILD

Put early versions of your product in the users' hands as soon as possible. Then watch what they do, and refine based on your observations.

CHAPTER THREE

SERVING YOUR CUSTOMERS

–

How to craft your customer service process for adoption, engagement, and delight

You've built it. Now the question is: Will they come? The rise of e-commerce and the social web has made finding customers for your product or service easier than ever. That said, it's also made it easier than ever for your customers to talk back.

Whereas brands used to push their products and messages out in what was essentially a one-way conversation, the social web has transformed it into a two-way conversation.

The impact is manifold: It means that we have to cultivate stories that create a real emotional connection to break through the noise. It means that we have to learn to speak authentically and honestly to our customers, and that we can't hide when we make mistakes. It means that we must strive not only to help our customers but also to inspire them.

Yet, no matter how fast-paced our world has become, some things never change. Like the fact that building relationships takes time. Trust and loyalty are not given; they are earned—little by little, tweet by tweet, delightful experience by delightful experience.

Which brings us to the real question, which is not "Will they come?" but rather "Are you ready to serve?"

RECRUITING AN ARMY
OF ALLIES

—

Chris Guillebeau

The blog post asking for donations went up with no preamble. There was no launch campaign and no guilt trip, just a simple description of the need for clean water in Ethiopia. The invitation to participate came at the end, asking readers to join in making a difference. In less than a day, $22,000 came in—all from the one post.

Another time, a launch for a commercial service went out to the same community. In the launch post and mailing, the campaign produced more than $100,000 in immediate income—all for a single product on a single day, from a relatively small audience.

I monitored the first campaign from a hotel room in Anchorage, Alaska, and the second took place in real time while riding an Amtrak train across the Midwest. In each case, I watched with wonder as the numbers on my laptop continued to increase. How did this happen?

You might think that these successes came from unusual circumstances. Maybe the post went viral, bringing in a deluge of outside visitors from big tech sites. But no—in each case, the donations, sales, and referrals were all driven by a small group of people. The message spread because invitations were widely shared by engaged individual readers.

The moment of trust came not in the arrival of a selected blog post or e-mail message, but in several years of relationship building that led up to each campaign. When the time came to garner funding or sell a product, it was a simple matter of activating that trust and issuing the invitations.

Such is the power of a small group of remarkable people, an army of allies who are eager to support a cause. Faster than a speeding bullet, more powerful than a Eurorail locomotive, and better than any paid advertising, an army of allies is the greatest asset you can cultivate. If you're just getting started and wondering where you should devote your focus, here's the answer: devote it to recruiting and serving these people.

STEP 1: INVITE YOUR ARMY TO SERVE

An army does not materialize out of nowhere or assemble on its own. The most important thing you can do to gain allies and attention is to produce good work. Take a stand—do something that matters! Next, make it clear that you welcome people to your mission. Give them something to believe in and a reason to care.

In a traditional army, the foot soldiers serve at the whim of commanders, and a clear hierarchy is maintained. But your charge, as the leader of your all-volunteer army, is essentially to serve. Every day, start by asking yourself two questions:

1. What am I making?

2. Whom am I helping?

Answering these questions—in word and deed—is crucial for the ongoing care and feeding of your army. For the past five years I've traveled the world, meeting people who identify with the message of nonconformity and unconventional living. Along the way, I've been inspired by hearing many of their stories. It's a continuous cycle of communication and connection, fueled by the belonging that comes from a common message.

STEP 2: IN TURN, SERVE YOUR ARMY

Years ago I heard someone use a phrase that's stuck with me ever since: "My marketing plan is strategic giving." That person, Megan Hunt, meant it in the context of her work as a blogger and fashion designer—her primary strategy for growth was relying on other bloggers to spread the word, and she often sent out free product in hopes of endorsements. But the lesson goes far beyond packaging up product and not including an invoice.

When you make the focus of your work what you can do for people instead of what they can do for you, you're not only being a good person; you're also building the loyalty of your small army.

Like relationships, loyalty isn't created in a single conversation or transaction. Instead, it's built over time. One of the best ways you can establish loyalty is through a series of touchstones—small things you repeatedly do that create a positive impact in someone's life. A few examples:

- **Make your expertise available to the community at regular intervals.** Pamela Slim, a coach and author, hosts a monthly "Ask Pam Anything" call-in session. She also does paid coaching calls, but the monthly session allows her to engage with people through a more informal channel. It builds trust in her expertise with the broader community and, no doubt, drives sales of paid sessions. But it's not just solopreneurs who can do this; businesses small and large have domain expertise that can be shared freely.

- **Share your paid content with users for free on different channels.** Attending the TED Conference, for example, comes at a premium ticket cost (and an invitation to boot), but TED also posts all the talks from the event for free online afterward. Enabling the talks to be freely shared allows brand awareness to grow and, ultimately, drives demand for tickets to the flagship live events.

- **Look around and be generally helpful wherever you can.**
  When in doubt, just ask what you can do. A year ago I initiated an experiment where I'd frequently go online (to Twitter, usually) and ask, "How can I help you?" Every time I posed this question I received a variety of responses. Some were silly or unreasonable, but I also learned a lot about my audience. It wasn't an academic exercise; whenever I conducted the experiment, I tried to do at least a few small things to actually help someone.

Reciprocity is a powerful practice. The more you give away, the stronger the bond you'll create with your army of allies. Strive to continually increase the percentage of your work that you make available to everyone, even as you block off other areas of your work that are available for sale or hire. Then, when it's finally time to ask for that sale, send that invoice, or request a higher fee, you'll have a reservoir of goodwill to draw on.

〜〜

Back in the dark ages when we all used dial-up, communities were explicitly local. If you wanted to connect with someone in another part of the world, your options were limited. These days, there's no doubt that the world has changed. You can now connect with people regardless of where they live. You can build a community based on mutual interests. You can deploy this community for social good, for profit, or in pursuit of a greater mission that combines the two. The key lies in crafting a consistent message, making a real difference in people's lives, and serving the people who've chosen to join your army.

Nothing is more important than your relationships with them. As with the $22,000 blog post or the $100,000 product launch, success is built on the creation of trust and value. If you make your army the focus of your daily work, rewards will inevitably follow.

CHRIS GUILLEBEAU is the New York Times *bestselling author of* The Happiness of Pursuit, The $100 Startup, *and other books. He visited every country in the world (193 in total) from 2002 to 2013. He writes about life, work, and travel on his Art of Non-Conformity blog.*

→ www.chrisguillebeau.com

"Put the customer first.

Invent. And be patient."

— JEFF BEZOS

ACTING (AND LISTENING)
LIKE A HUMAN BEING

—

Sean Blanda

Think about all the tone-deaf customer service interactions you've had. The ones where you were treated like a stepping-stone to profit rather than an actual human. The tech support person telling you to restart your computer as he reads a script, the airline attendant throwing up her hands and telling you, "There's nothing I can do," the bureaucrat refusing to even consider your problem until you've filled out all the right forms. Chances are you only interact with companies like these when you have no other choice. And that's why they're not going to last.

Because they forgot that the person standing in front of them is the reason they have a job in the first place, and that listening to that person and making his life easier should be priority #1.

Your customer is someone who spends hours at his or her job away from friends and family to earn a paycheck. One of the things they choose to do with part of that paycheck is willingly give it to you, a complete stranger that they will likely never meet, because that thing you make is just so great they think the trade-off is worth it.

Your job? Instill enough trust and respect in the customer that they are willing to make that leap. And then do it again. And again. This isn't easy, and too many of the stories we hear gloss over this long and hard (and extremely rewarding) task, instead perpetuating the start-up myth that the point of business is getting to the end: raising funds, cashing out, and stepping down to sip daiquiris on a beach somewhere.

But priming your business for the end is not only less fun; it's bad business strategy. Building a sustainable business starts with making respect for your customers a sacred value. It also often means taking steps that don't quite make sense in the short term—at least at first.

PLAY THE LONG GAME

Perhaps the best modern example of maniacal customer focus is Amazon. To customers, Amazon is known for its low prices and friendly shipping policies. But to Wall Street, it is known as the company that refuses to actually turn a substantial profit. Why? Because it invests any extra cash into lowering prices, expanding infrastructure, and developing long-term projects (like the Kindle) that make customers happy.

In his first letter to shareholders in 1997, CEO Jeff Bezos made his tactics clear: "We will continue to focus relentlessly on our customers. We will continue to make investment decisions in light of long-term market leadership considerations rather than short-term profitability considerations or short-term Wall Street reactions."

Amazon waited four years—the equivalent of a century in start-up time—to move beyond selling just books, instead rolling out innovations like 1-Click Shopping and adding fulfillment centers for faster shipping. In other words, it focused on listening to and pleasing customers before growth, and that took a long time to get right. By 2013, *Bloomberg Businessweek* reported, "In the meantime, investors are happy to sit and watch the company grow faster than the rest of e-commerce."

But Amazon's eventual—and startlingly rapid—growth was only possible because it focused on getting the customer experience right from the start.

"DO THINGS THAT DON'T SCALE"

Today, Airbnb is practically a household name, not to mention one of the key catalysts behind the rise of the "sharing economy." But the company wasn't always riding high.

Back in 2009, the company was stuck, spinning its wheels. The idea behind the business was to allow anyone to list a spare bedroom or apartment for nightly rental. This type of platform is what's known as a double-sided marketplace, which requires a critical mass of both buyers (those who want to rent) and sellers (those who want to let their places) to be successful. But the customers weren't showing up. As co-founder Joe Gebbia describes it, Airbnb's web traffic was in "the Midwest of analytics—everything was flat."

The start-up was based in the Valley and belonged to one of the country's marquee incubators, Y Combinator. In other words, the young founders were at ground zero for the "scale fast" ethos that pervades modern business culture. According to Gebbia, the turning point came when their advisor Paul Graham gave them some counterintuitive advice: He encouraged them to "do things that don't scale."

Graham's logic was that Airbnb had to get the service perfect for its first few customers before it could even think about growing. To do that, Gebbia and co-founder Brian Chesky decided to go on the road and experience the product just like their customers. So they started staying in Airbnb rentals, while hosting meet-ups in whatever city they were staying in. They got to know their early adopters and understand their needs.

They also had some fun. Says Chesky, "I've stayed with one of the top air guitarists in San Francisco, also a guy who is the #2 ranked Skee-Ball champion in the US." They learned firsthand what would make their customers' lives easier and put faces to the listings on their site.

"We met our community one by one, and they gave us insights about what was broken. Then we iterated like crazy," says Gebbia. The result? As of 2014, the service operates in thirty-five thousand cities, has served eleven million guests, and is valued at $10 billion.

REMOVE PAIN POINTS

Of course, you don't have to be a tech company to adopt a customer-first mind-set. Consider Charles Schwab, a business that's been quietly innovating for decades in the banking and investment industry.

Charles Schwab has no physical locations, and there's no decorated lobby you can visit to open your account. Instead, the company chooses to spend that money on delivering incredible service. Schwab was the first brokerage firm to offer stock quotes twenty-four hours a day by phone. It offers ATM cards that refund any fees, no matter if you have $10 in your account or $10,000. When you call customer service, there is no phone tree. You go directly to an actual human. When they answer, the agent on the other end lets you know where they are located ("Hello, this is Mike in Minneapolis")—no outsourced help with awkwardly Anglicized names.

Schwab addresses the actual pain points of its customers. Rather than put profit before customer service, the company puts customer service before profit, intuiting that one will follow from the other.

~∞~

Don't treat your customers like a "1" in the page view column or as money to be tucked into a budget document. They'll know. Amazon made their customers' lives easier, and they came back in droves. Airbnb listened to their customers one by one and took their feedback to heart, and the business's growth skyrocketed. Charles Schwab identified what every single customer hates about banking (hidden fees) and removed them.

But being human is more than just a good policy. It's more fun. No one starts a business with the intention of sitting alone in a room staring at a glowing screen all day. We start businesses to make the lives of those around us better or easier (and earn a little scratch in the process).

Nothing is more rewarding than launching a new product or service you believe in and then asking your customers to help make it better. I've never spoken with a longtime entrepreneur who attributed success to keeping his or her head down and listening to no one.

Every time someone lands on your website or purchases your product, they're raising their hand and letting you know that they care. We'd be wise to return the favor. Listen to your customers, no matter how much it slows you down.

SEAN BLANDA is the managing editor of 99U, where he writes often about the future of careers, especially in regard to young people. He is also the co-founder of Philly Tech Week and Technical.ly, a network of news sites that cover East Coast technology communities. Sean is known to enjoy a good Twitter argument.

→ Follow him @SeanBlanda

"Attention is the rarest and purest form of generosity."

— SIMONE WEIL

Q&A:

INSTILLING CONFIDENCE
EVERY STEP OF THE WAY

—

with Neil Blumenthal

Founded in 2010, lifestyle brand Warby Parker
has been wildly successful from day one. They
launched with editorials in *Vogue* and *GQ* and sold
out of their top fifteen eyewear styles in a matter
of weeks, racking up a waiting list of more than
twenty thousand customers. Since then, they've
raised more than $100 million in funding; grown to
more than three hundred employees; and launched
brick-and-mortar spaces in New York, Los Angeles,
and Boston. Not to mention being one of the most
talked-about brands on the social web. We chatted
with co-founder and co-CEO Neil Blumenthal about
the secret sauce behind Warby Parker's resound-
ing success and their strategy for inspiring confidence with customers every step of the way.

Where do you think brands go wrong when they're trying to build an authentic relationship with customers?

People have extremely sensitive BS detectors these days. We've all been inundated with advertisements since we started walking and talking. So we can pick up on a brand's authenticity—or fakeness—immediately. As a brand, you can only engender trust if you're being transparent. Brands have never been able to control what their customers say about them, but now, thanks to the Internet, customers are more empowered than ever to disseminate their experiences with a brand. Companies can't hide. If you make a mistake, or you do something wrong, it's going to get out there. And if you're not proactive about responding when it happens, you're going to dig yourself into a deeper hole.

What's the best way to go about being "proactive" when something goes wrong?

I think it goes back to transparency. The first thing to do is admit it. Explain what happened and apologize. Your customers can be very understanding provided that you enable them to be understanding, which means that you need to have an honest discussion with them and fess up when you make a mistake.

For instance, think about if you call any of our favorite cell phone carriers. [*laughs*] It used to be that they were just rude and didn't solve your problem. Now, they're often polite, but they still don't solve your problems. So, they're getting a little bit better, but you still want to break your phone in half after one of those conversations.

So being polite and friendly and apologizing is part of it. But it's just the first part. Then you have to actually correct the situation. For us, that might be offering a discount, it might be offering free glasses, it might be doing whatever it takes to get that person a pair of glasses before they go on vacation. It's the little things that make a brand great. It's about being diligent with details, keeping your antennae sensitive to what customers want, and responding in a way that's authentic to your brand. It sounds intuitive, but the fact is that many brands are not treating their customers the way they want to be treated.

Do you think the dynamic of the social web means there's more of an interplay between customers and brands than there's been in the past? Can brands still control the conversation?

I was talking to Troy Carter—an investor who also used to be Lady Gaga's manager—the other day, and he made a really interesting observation. We were discussing Warby Parker, and he said, "It's not your brand; it's our brand." "Our" being the public. And I think he's right: You do not control your brand anymore. You can influence it and help guide the conversation, but there's a limit to how precisely you can define your brand on your own.

This idea that a brand will conform to a nice PowerPoint presentation with a strict brand architecture and messaging hierarchy is no longer the case. Your brand is part of conversations that are being had in the streets, on Twitter, and on Instagram. And the best that you can do is help influence that dialogue by giving people reasons to talk positively about it. These days, your community managers are your brand managers.

What are the values that you strive to instill in your customer service team?

The first thing is the need to be empathetic and the importance of being friendly, super-friendly. Now, we can't teach them how to be friendly, of course; that's something that we try to identify during the interview process. But one thing that we can teach in training is how to take pride in being friendly, and how to view a difficult situation as a challenge, where you strive to resolve it so that you're happy and the customer is happy. So, essentially, taking pride in turning a negative experience for a customer into a positive one.

You've spoken before about this notion of great customer service as "inspiring confidence" every step of the way. How does that play out in terms of strategy at Warby Parker?

I think it goes back to really understanding the customer and how they make decisions. With buying glasses, we found that people cared first about how they looked, second about price, third about quality and customer service, and fourth about social mission. When you look at the hierarchy of messages that we put out there, it leads with fashion, then price, then service, and finally our social mission. Our mission is extremely robust and really motivates us, but we recognize that it's not what drives someone to buy a pair of glasses from us.

So I think the question really is: How do you continue to instill confidence throughout the process that this is the right decision and the right move? If you think about Apple, their marketing strategy is about inspiring confidence every step of the way. When you go on the website, you think, "Wow this is really is the best product for X, Y, and Z reasons." Then when you get an iPhone, for instance, and take it out of the box, you see that it's not jammed in there; it's not difficult to get out, nor does it fall out. It just sort of slides out into your hand at exactly the right speed. You may not think about it consciously, but that whole process is giving you confidence that this is going to be a good product.

At Warby Parker, we're always thinking about the steps that will instill confidence. Having a beautiful site and a beautiful shopping experience is certainly one. You want your site to be fast and easy to use. But beyond that, there are many more cues.

For us, offering free shipping and free returns is one. Sure, the customer recognizes that it will save her money, but hopefully what it's also communicating is the idea that we believe so much in our product that we know you are going to like it. Therefore, it's actually profitable for us to pay for free shipping and free returns because you're not going to need to return your glasses.

NEIL BLUMENTHAL loves helping people see. He is co-founder and co-CEO of Warby Parker, a lifestyle brand offering designer eyewear at a revolutionary price while leading the way for socially conscious business. For every pair of glasses sold, a pair is distributed to someone in need.

→ www.warbyparker.com

"Everybody is interesting when they are interested in something."

— AMY POEHLER

INVITING YOUR CUSTOMERS INTO YOUR STORY

—

Craig Dalton

Have you ever taken the time to tell your friends about a product, review it, tweet or Facebook about it? I'm not talking about lashing out on Twitter with a complaint for a quick customer service response, but rather taking the time to leave an unsolicited compliment for a product or service you love. Or how about sharing the story behind a brand and why you care about it with your circle of friends? Sure, it's easy to surface this kind of product love with social media now, but what drew out these public displays of love in the first place?

The answer is simple. It's the thing that has driven man since time eternal: stories. Entrepreneurs and creators alike are figuring out that their products are more than the materials and designs that go into them. At their best, the products we love become a part of the fabric of our lives. They become part of the stories that we tell ourselves about how we want to work smarter, dream bigger, and build a better world. They evoke an emotional connection—and a vocal, engaged, and loyal community naturally emerges.

You'll be surprised by just how much that community can do: they can spread the word about your company, provide almost instantaneous product feedback, and even begin servicing other members of the community. Patagonia has done it. Nest has done it. My company did it. And so can you.

GREAT STORIES INSPIRE US

Founded in 1973 by mountain climber Yvon Chouinard, Patagonia has become one of the most iconic outdoor apparel companies in the world by being a story-driven company. While Patagonia has its roots in rock and alpine climbing, for most customers these activities are a rarity. They don't know who climbing greats Tommy Caldwell and Lynn Hill are, and they may never summit a mountain peak in their lifetimes.

But that doesn't matter. Because Patagonia activates our aspirations—our ambition to travel to faraway places, to push beyond our boundaries, to commit feats of daring we never thought we could. From their name to the majestic outdoor photography that's ever present in their marketing, Patagonia taps into our dreams of adventure and achievement.

The brand also inspires us, not just to do more but to do better. Patagonia was one of the first companies to donate a fixed portion of its profits to the preservation of the environment through its "1% for the Planet" initiative launched in 1985. They also pioneered one of the first "postconsumer recycled" lines in 1993, creating a new product line woven from a polyester fiber made from recycled plastic bottles.

With Patagonia, where your jacket comes from, and what you imagine you might do while wearing it, are a natural part of the product experience. The story, and the emotional connection, are built right in.

–

Ask yourself: *How are you tapping into your audience's aspirations and dreams?*

GREAT STORIES CHANGE THE WAY WE THINK

Now, let's take a look at Nest, the "smart home" company that was acquired by Google for $3.2 billion in 2014. Before Nest introduced its learning thermostat in 2011, when was the last time you ever thought about the "design" of your thermostat? Or how helpful it would be to be able to control it remotely? Probably never.

Nest co-founder and CEO Tony Fadell took his years of learning from playing a key role in the industrial design group at Apple and applied them to a home product category no one was talking about. The simplicity and beauty of the designs for Nest's learning thermostat, and, later, its Protect smoke alarm, transformed these neglected objects into coveted home essentials.

What's more, they utterly changed the way we thought about the products themselves and what we needed. With the thermostat,

Nest told us a story about being better stewards of our environment and saving money by having a product that learned about our HVAC habits. With the Protect, Nest told us that "safety shouldn't be annoying"—why should we helplessly wave a broom in front of our smoke alarms, when new technologies could allow us to silence it with the wave of a hand? They connected us with our homes in a way the rest of the industry never thought possible—and they did it by thinking differently.

–

Ask yourself: *How is my product going to change the way people think or go about their daily lives?*

GREAT STORIES START CONVERSATIONS

When we think of stories, we usually think of something with a beginning, a middle, and an end. But in today's hyperconnected world, your story can't stop with a tagline. If you want to truly engage an audience, you have to, well, truly engage with them; that means making them a part of the ever-evolving conversation about your brand.

I know this because I've experienced it firsthand with my own company, DODOcase. We founded the company in 2010 with the tagline "Protects from Extinction" the day the original Apple iPad was launched. We believed that as consumers further embraced e-readers and tablet computers, that the art of traditional bookbinding was at risk of disappearing. So we designed a tablet case using traditional bookbinding materials and techniques that leveraged San Francisco's bookbinding talent.

So what's up with our name? We wanted one that was easy to remember—quirky and meaningful. We wanted something that evoked a response even in the absence of knowing anything about what we did. We arrived at DODOcase as an homage to the flightless dodo bird. We found that most people had heard of the dodo although many couldn't remember why. A small minority would remember the dodo as the most famously referenced example of an extinct animal. (Bonus fact: A shipwrecked Dutch sailor on the Mauritius Islands reported the last known dodo bird in 1662.) The name represented our desire to protect the art of bookbinding from extinction and to protect your new iPad.

Since we were a bootstrapped company, we knew from the get-go that we would have to infuse our story into everything we did. We wanted to foster a genuine appreciation and connection with the San Francisco–based craftsmen and craftswomen that make all our products. And we wanted, even needed, our customers to appreciate this fact.

During our first six months, if you wanted a DODOcase, you'd have to wait about six weeks to get one because of the small scale of our manufacturing resources relative to the demand we created. And our San Francisco–based manufacturing meant our products cost a premium to boot. In this must-have-it-delivered-tomorrow world we live in, we were asking people to patiently wait well over a month to encase their beloved iPads—and at a higher cost than some competitors.

But our backlog turned out to be an unexpected boon. While we were spending all our time binding books and sanding bamboo trays in an attempt to get products out the door, something amazing was happening online. Our customers were talking about us while they waited. They would tweet when they placed the order. Then they would retweet us when we would send out updates of our progress. Then they would post pictures once the product had arrived. This patience was a result of us allowing them to take part in our journey.

We fueled this action every day. It wasn't difficult, and it was entirely free. If my business partner, Patrick, was carrying a sheet of bamboo on his back covered in sawdust—I took a picture and posted it to Twitter and Facebook. If we had a stack of DODOcases that we were boxing to ship, I'd post a picture. The closer our customers felt to our process, it seemed, the more they loved us. And love, in today's connected age, goes a long way.

—

Ask yourself: *How can you share more of the process behind your product with customers? It can be good, bad, or ugly—as long as it's honest.*

CRAIG DALTON *is CEO and co-founder of DODOcase, a founding member of SF Made, and a champion of the local manufacturing movement around the country. He can be found on Twitter @one1speed.*

→ www.dodocase.com

"Give, give, give, give, give... Ask."

— GARY VAYNERCHUK

FOCUSING ON "SMALL KINDNESSES"

—

Shane Snow

"It's easy to miss the real point of our lives even as we're living them," writes Arianna Huffington in her book *Thrive*. "And it is very telling what we don't hear in eulogies." Those things include making senior vice president, sacrificing kids' Little League games to go over those numbers one more time, or my personal favorite: "she dealt with every email in her inbox every night."

"You never hear, 'George increased market share by 30 percent,'" Huffington said at a recent event at Soho House in New York City. What you do hear in eulogies, she says, are stories of "small kindnesses."

It's well known that details make good art great. Subtle word choices separate great poets from amateurs. Small flourishes define superlative architecture. Tiny considerations make products world-class ("Jobs spent days agonizing over just how rounded the corners should be," writes Walter Isaacson about the Apple II in *Steve Jobs*).

I think the same can be said about building a great business. Tiny considerations in the interactions companies have with their customers are all about focusing on people before profits—and, paradoxically, this can yield huge returns. This is the mentality that Wharton professor Adam Grant talks about in his research on corporate "givers" versus "takers." In various now-famous studies in his book *Give and Take*, Grant has shown that the most successful people in the workplace tend to be the ones who give selflessly to others without expectation of returned favors. Research by Jim Stengel, former global marketing head at Procter & Gamble, shows that this also works at a corporate level. Businesses "center[ed] on improving people's lives outperform their competitors," he writes, after studying a decade of market performance of fifty thousand brands.

In *Thrive*, Huffington argues that power and money have too long been life's main yardsticks of success, and that we should measure our achievements instead by four new metrics: Wisdom, Wonder, Well-Being, and Giving. If the eulogy test is an indication, Giving is likely the most memorable of the four.

"It's tempting to reserve the giver label for larger-than-life heroes such as Mother Teresa or Mahatma Gandhi, but being a giver doesn't require extraordinary acts of sacrifice," Grant writes in *Give and Take*. "It just involves a focus on acting in the interests of others."

I experienced this giver philosophy recently when I was shopping for—of all things—temporary tattoos. My search led me to a website called Tattly, which sells fancy stick-on tattoos and was created by a designer named Tina Roth Eisenberg (commonly known as the Swissmiss). I put the fox tattoo two-pack I was looking for (don't ask me why the eccentric hunt for such a thing) in my shopping cart, and checked out.

A few days later, an envelope from Tattly came, containing not two but four temporary tattoos: two foxes and two of another design. At first, I thought this was a packing error in my favor, but when I looked into it, sure enough, these are freebies that Tattly gives to every one of its customers. When I asked Eisenberg about it, she said, "From the very start, we always gave an extra Tattly away in every order. It's a simple way to delight our customers."

The cost of sending two free tattoos with every order is negligible. The materials themselves cost Tattly a few cents, the shipping cost remains the same (stick-on tattoos weigh nothing), and the labor cost is minimal. But it virtually ensures that customers return. Even if you don't want extra tattoos, the fact that Tattly gives them to you makes you like the company.

The free tattoos aren't the only small kindnesses tucked in the folds of Tattly's business. They're a symptom of an overarching philosophy. "I want to sell something I love to people that love it," Eisenberg says. "I want my customers to have a smile on their face." The bottom of the company's "About Us" page reads, "P.S. You look great today!" Eisenberg says, "Every now and then we get an e-mail or tweet pointing out that it made someone smile." Its product envelopes are decorated with stickers and use real postage stamps instead of printed business postage. The FAQ page answers the question, "How far is the Big Dipper from the earth?" And Eisenberg recently redesigned the Tattly invoice to make it pretty and a little bit funny. "Most people wouldn't even give an invoice design another thought," she says. "But I do. It's another way to communicate with our customer."

To some businesspeople, these small considerations may seem like small inefficiencies, but to businesses like Tattly, they're investments in customers. Two and a half years since launch, Tattly has a team of ten and ships four hundred designs around the world to shops like J.Crew, Urban Outfitters, and the MoMA Design Store. And companies like GE, Twitter, and NPR buy custom tattoos from Tattly by the thousands.

When I look at other fast-growing companies with voracious users, I see small kindnesses everywhere. Uber recently upped the ante for me on car services when I got into one of its town cars in San Francisco. The driver had placed fancy jars of candies in the console for passengers. It was a small thing, but somehow it made me feel like the most important customer in the world. I gave him five stars. Tumblr's terms of service reflect a culture of fun and user-centeredness: they use plain English and colloquialisms and throw in humor to make the read bearable. Few people read terms of service, and Tumblr doesn't have to do this; they do it because they care about the little things. Google has famously kept its home page to a minimum number of words (currently I see sixteen, mostly the header and footer) in order to respect users' time and not distract from the one thing they want: search. And Google periodically brings smiles to our faces by replacing its logo with themed "Doodles" on special occasions, such as the fiftieth anniversary of *Dr. Who* or *Frankenstein* author Mary Shelley's birthday.

This is a huge departure from the paradigm that's dominated business for the last century. Instead of focusing on themselves, thoughtful companies are now asking what Eisenberg asks: "How can I put a smile on my audience's face, in lieu of getting in their face?"

If I had my way, every business would adopt the manifesto that's painted on the front wall of the Manhattan office of my friends at NextJump.com. The block letters read, "Our Mission: Do all the little things, so that others can do the things they were meant to do." Free tattoos, fun "About Us" pages and invoices, plainspoken terms of service, and smile-inducing logo hacks are small investments, especially when compared with the costs of customer acquisition through advertising. But these kindnesses pay big dividends and are some of the ways new companies can hack the ladder to credibility and customer success in a short time. As Dr. Grant says, the more they give, the more successful they are. Indeed, a culture of tiny kindnesses isn't just good for the world. It's good for business.

SHANE SNOW is the chief creative officer of Contently (www. contently.com) and a technology journalist whose work has appeared in Wired, Fast Company, *the* New Yorker, *and many others. Named one of* Details Magazine's *"Digital Mavericks" and* Forbes's *30 Under 30 Media Innovators, he's the author of* Smartcuts: How Hackers, Innovators, and Icons Accelerate Success.

→ www.shanesnow.com

KEY
TAKEAWAYS

–

Serving Your Customers

Get more insights and the desktop wallpaper at:

→ www.99u.com/customers

- ## MAKE STORYTELLING SECOND NATURE
  Build a story into your brand from day one. Then, invite customers into that story by using the social web to share your thinking, your challenges, and your successes.

- ## PLAY THE LONG GAME
  Get to know your customers—and their pain points—early on, even if it requires tactics that aren't sustainable. You have to perfect the customer experience before you can scale.

- ## FREE UP YOUR EXPERTISE
  Make reciprocity part of your business strategy. Strive to share some part of your expertise, content, or product with your community for free.

- ## CONVERSATION IS A TWO-WAY STREET
  Don't try to control the conversation about your brand. Focus instead on influencing the conversation your customers are having in a positive way by delivering killer service.

- ## REFINE YOUR PROCESS TO IMPRESS
  Consider all the cues—big and small—that you can use to instill confidence in your customer as you build out your service process.

- ## DELIGHT IS IN THE DETAILS
  Don't forget to have fun, and imbue your brand experience with "small kindnesses." Customers notice the little things; no detail is too small to be an opportunity for delight.

CHAPTER FOUR

LEADING YOUR TEAM

—

*How to step up, keep your team
on track, and inspire greatness*

In an era where initiative and innovation are what we prize most, leadership is the opposite of what many of us think it is: Telling people what to do. The true leader's job is to help everyone around them do their job better.

It's about letting go of an "I-know-best" perspective and instead giving your team all of the agency and information they need to take responsibility into their own hands and act.

Of course, this is easier said than done. Particularly for creatives, who can be fond of dismissing leadership as something that other people do. To rally those with a maker (not manager) mind-set to our cause, we kick off this chapter with a look at why managing a team is a rare and valuable skill worth cultivating, and why creatives are uniquely suited to lead in this time of rapid change.

Then we dig into the essentials of great leadership: how to drive better collaboration by upping your commitment to transparency, how to make sure everyone is communicating and moving forward in unison, and how to instill ownership and pride in your team members.

Every great business needs someone standing at the helm, guiding the ship. So if you truly want to make an impact, it's time to get your sea legs.

GETTING RID OF "RELUCTANT MANAGER SYNDROME"

—

Rich Armstrong

Managers are under fire these days. And it's no wonder. From *Dilbert* to *Office Space*, we all know the trope of the useless and conniving political player who's managed to entrench himself into an otherwise well-meaning organization. He holds the keys to advancement, adds little value, makes other people miserable, and seeks only more power.

But I believe that the pointy-haired bosses and the Bill Lumberghs are not a natural by-product of doing business. Rather, they are a natural by-product of companies that refuse to take good management seriously. They're indicative of an organization that cares too much about what they're doing and not enough about how they're doing it.

In start-ups, this attitude toward management typically manifests itself in the unspoken assumption: "We can't do this well, so we're not going to do it at all."

This is otherwise known as focusing on your core competency, and it's a valuable and necessary strength of any start-up. But, as Zingerman's co-founder Ari Weinzweig, one of my favorite business thinkers, has said:

> *Whatever your strengths are, they will likely lead straight into your weaknesses.*

By definition, great start-ups excel at staying focused, outsourcing, offloading, abstracting problems. It's no surprise that they look at this big messy challenge of management and think: "How can we avoid doing this at all?" And it's fine to do that with your Linux servers or your fancy catered lunch, but it's not OK to do it with leadership.

Why? Because a dismissive attitude toward leadership is exactly what makes us end up with bad managers in the first place. When you decline an opportunity to lead, you open up a vacuum for other people to take on management roles, sometimes the very people you set out to avoid. What's more, you're essentially leaving the happiness and productivity of your team to the whims of fate.

WHY SHOULD WE PAY ATTENTION TO MANAGEMENT?

My revelation about the purpose of good management came years ago in the home of Chuck Newman. A close family friend, a wonderful host, and a longtime corporate and community leader, Chuck was like an uncle to me when I was growing up.

At Christmas dinner in 2005, Chuck said something that changed my life. While we were catching up, he asked how things were going with my career at Google. The company was growing fast and hiring lots of top-notch people, but above and around me I saw mostly conniving and striving. No one cared about the people doing real work. Everyone cared only about getting ahead.

Chuck asked if I ever wanted to be a manager. I dismissed the idea with a wave of my hand and said that managers were useless. That I'd rather focus on something important. I said this to a man whose success in management had paid for the rib roast I was eating and the wine I was drinking. But Chuck reacted in a characteristically good-natured way. "Really?" he said. "I'm surprised by that." Then he said the thing that changed my life:

> *I've always thought that the hardest and most valuable thing in work is to get a group of smart people to work together toward a common goal.*

It blew my mind. As soon as Chuck framed management as something that's very hard and very valuable, I started to think about it differently. This was like telling a certain type of coder that Haskell is hard, a certain type of gamer that *Dwarf Fortress* is hard, or a certain type of athlete that CrossFit is hard. I just couldn't let it go.

The idea stuck with me throughout my remaining time at Google, but opportunities to lead were mostly being given to outside hires. So I started looking elsewhere. Eventually, I saw the chance to found the customer support team at Fog Creek Software. The company's ideals spoke to me. I got to build a team from scratch, attracting and mentoring a continual stream of talented folks. I joined Fog Creek because I wanted to help people (i.e., our customers). And as my team has grown to thirty-plus employees, including sales, marketing, and product development, I still see my job as helping people.

BEING A SERVANT LEADER, NOT AN EAGER LEADER

What I've learned through this process is that leadership isn't about power or control or hierarchy; it's about serving. If you really want to get people fired up and get them to excel, your practices have to be grounded in the idea of "servant leadership." It's really the only sane way to run a company.

Clayton Christensen says it best in *How Will You Measure Your Life?*:

> I used to think that if you cared for other people,
> you need to study sociology or something like it . . .
> I concluded, if you want to help other people, be a
> manager. If done well, management is among the
> most noble of professions.

I don't have to be a manager. I went to Sarah Lawrence College to be a novelist. I've held almost every position in software development. I can code (but probably shouldn't). But all of those things, however exciting, lack the core component of helping people directly. Specific people. Not humanity, not a disenfranchised class of people, but individuals I can see and understand. To me, it's the only thing I have done professionally that gives me more than it asks of me—and thus is sustainable.

The people in my industry—the tech industry—need little prompting to abdicate their responsibility to lead. Many analytical types are already ill-suited to the task, given their distaste for messiness and gray areas. I felt this way, too, when I was younger.

Management is, at least initially, not an attractive job to the people who should be doing it. But leadership acumen and a good heart are what are needed most everywhere. And especially where good leadership has been left to the default, to the pull of charisma, to the machinations of the power broker.

The pointy-haired bosses? The Bill Lumberghs? They're what you get if you don't treat management both seriously and with a measure of healthy skepticism. They're what you get when your managers are eager to manage. A flat organization is a hundred-dollar bill laying on the sidewalk to these people. To a charismatic sociopath, or a good old-fashioned schemer, an organization without good servant leaders is like a field of wheat to a locust. In short, good management culture is your immune system against douche bags.

If you care about the people around you and you cede the responsibility to become a leader, you are—every day—effectively promoting a new d-bag into management. I'm not saying you should storm into your boss's office and demand to be promoted to management. That never works.

But when good people start learning about servant leadership, something wonderful happens. The people around them start sighing with relief. Finally! Someone has taken on the challenge.

So go. Learn about it. Start getting comfortable with the idea of being a manager. It's exactly what we need. You are exactly who we need.

RICH ARMSTRONG proudly wears the title of general manager at Fog Creek Software, maker of the online tools FogBugz, Kiln, and Trello.

→ Follow him on Twitter at @richarmstrong

"Leadership is not a position, leadership is a choice."

— SIMON SINEK

MAKING TRANSPARENCY AN ESSENTIAL PART OF YOUR CULTURE

—

Joel Gascoigne

As of February 2014, there were 1,320,813 people signed up for my product. 129,855 of those people actively use the product each month, and in January 2014 we generated a total of $325,000 in revenue. My salary is $163,000. Our blog received 654,126 unique visitors in the last month, and we answered 9,771 customer support e-mails. We have $361,000 in the bank and no current plans to raise further funding since the $450,000 seed round we raised in December 2011, for which we gave up 14 percent of the company. All of this data is available to my team of eighteen, as well as to the public.

At my company, Buffer, we approach everything with a mind-set to "Default to transparency," which means that we ask, "Why not be open about this?" with everything we do. We share salary and equity numbers with the team. Any e-mails among team members are cc'd to mailing lists so the whole company can click a label and see every conversation and discussion happening. Even external e-mail conversations we have around marketing and press are bcc'd to lists so that team members can learn how we approach these tasks.

If I meet with an investor, the team knows about that, too. We have a shared Dropbox folder with all our seed round investment documents and other information. Everyone in the team knows that they can mention any details to someone interested in how we approach customer support, marketing, product development or our vision, goals, and current metrics. People are often drawn to Buffer because of our openness, and, because we share many of our processes and motivations publicly, we're able to attract and hire people who are a natural cultural fit.

TRANSPARENCY AS A CATALYST

Transparency is interesting because there are some incredible benefits that are simply denied to you completely if you choose to hide information. And it turns out that these very things are the most essential ingredients for innovation and collaboration—the lifeblood of twenty-first-century businesses.

1. Transparency breeds trust, and trust is the foundation of great teamwork. I believe that increased trust is the most fundamental and powerful reason to choose to adopt a culture of transparency. Imagine someone joins your company and negotiates hard for a higher salary. Someone who didn't negotiate so aggressively learns about it in a lunch conversation and quickly becomes envious. These kinds of politics occupy peoples' minds and quickly make a team unproductive. When details such as individual compensation, revenue, and profitability are kept secret, it is hard to trust one another. When everything is completely open, you can see that the company has been thoughtful and fair. The team can then become focused on a common goal and get to work.

2. Sharing all information is essential to innovation. As managers and leaders, we all want to empower our team members to act with initiative and purpose. We are looking for people who can take an idea and follow through from concept to reality in the same way we would have done it, or ideally even better. The surprising thing, however, is that the default for most companies is to keep the most salient information for decision making a secret. Keith Rabois, an experienced entrepreneur who has held executive roles at PayPal, LinkedIn, and Square, argues that if you want people to make smart decisions, they need full context and all the available information. Put simply, you can't expect people to make the decisions you would make without all the information that you have.

3. With openness, you attract loyalty. The benefits of transparency extend to your customers, users, readers, viewers, and future audience, too. When you start sharing the details of your business and decision processes, you make yourself more human. When you share failures as well as successes, people know that you're doing everything you can to make customers happy. Doing this consistently over time develops incredible trust and loyalty. People know that you "have their back" and not only will they be much less likely to jump to a competitor; they will also become vocal supporters and friends, bringing new customers.

4. Transparency leads to fairness and responsibility. By sharing compensation openly within the team, you make it clear that you are dedicated to being fair. John Mackey, co-founder and co-chief executive officer of Whole Foods Markets, a company with compensation transparency, reasons that "any kind of favoritism or nepotism is seen" at his organization as a result. This leads to a "greater justice" in compensation. At Buffer, we built on top of that, and have a formula for salary that is based on role, experience level, location, and seniority. We believe this is a big step forward in fighting against compensation inequality.

5. Transparency allows you to gain invaluable feedback. Becoming committed to a culture of openness is not easy, but it can be approached one step at a time and the benefits are quite incredible. One of the hardest parts of transparency is to share the "why" behind your decisions with the knowledge that others will see this and may criticize you. Putting it all out there can be scary, but it's also hugely rewarding. Team members will weigh in with their ideas for how to improve all aspects of the business. You will also hold yourself to a higher standard, since you know that you will share the details of everything you do.

HOW TO GET STARTED

At Buffer, we've had a commitment to transparency over an extended period of time and have continued to build on our existing efforts. It might not make sense in every scenario to go as far as we have with becoming transparent, but there are a few simple practices you can easily experiment with:

- **Share some e-mail conversations company-wide.** There are likely to be quite a number of e-mail conversations happening within teams in your company. Try having people cc a list, which everyone in the team has access to, when they write these e-mails. This is something we learned from Stripe, the successful web and mobile payments company. This simple change could have a profound impact on team cohesion, communication, and trust.

- **Take an internal monthly or quarterly report and make it public.** Take something like your monthly marketing report, for example. It might feel scary to share the report in its exact form (i.e., with numbers such as unique visitors or the number of conversions from marketing efforts to paying customers), so you could also try cutting a few details out of the first one and see whether you feel comfortable including them in future content. You'll be surprised how interested customers and team members in other departments are in learning about the decisions made. For some inspiration based on how we do this, take a look at open.bufferapp.com.

- **Share meeting notes and slide decks with everyone.** At Jack Dorsey's company Square, every meeting with more than two employees requires note taking, and the notes are shared with the rest of the six-hundred-plus person company. You can try this in your company in a simple way to begin with by sharing a specific category of meetings. This approach keeps meetings focused on real work and action points, and it means that the whole company is aware of new developments and can make suggestions.

People often ask me if there's anything I would change about our transparent approach if I could go back. The only thing I can think of is that I wish we had done it sooner. As soon as you start making adjustments toward being more transparent, you'll find out how valued this openness is by employees and customers. It's also surprisingly liberating.

JOEL GASCOIGNE is the founder and CEO of Buffer, the simplest and most powerful social media tool. He writes, speaks, and tweets about transparency, company culture, and customer happiness. Find him on Twitter at @joelgascoigne.

→ www.joel.is

"Decide what you stand for. And then stand for it all the time."

— CLAYTON CHRISTENSEN

Q&A:

REFRAMING LEADERSHIP FROM A MAKER'S PERSPECTIVE

—

with John Maeda

With advanced degrees in design, computer science, and business, John Maeda's education seems custom-designed to put him in the catbird seat for the start-up revolution. Couple that with thirteen years as head of research at the MIT Media Lab, six years as president of the Rhode Island School of Design, and his current role as design guru at a renowned venture firm, and, well, you've got someone who knows a little bit about working with—and leading—creative risk-takers from all walks of life. We picked Maeda's brain about why some creative folks don't like the idea of leadership, and why they may be more suited to it than they think.

The transition from maker to leader is a big challenge for many creative people. What do you think that's about?

When you make things with your hands, you force something into being. You sand it, you cut it, you fold it . . . You do everything to build it from end to end. Whereas leading requires a lot of talking, a lot of communicating—not using your hands. And when you're a creative who makes things, you immediately build a distinction between the talkers and the makers. And makers tend to look down on talkers. And leaders are talkers. You don't trust them, but now you're one of them. [laughs] At first you think you can't make anything with your hands anymore. But you can. You make relationships. One at a time. With the same painstaking attention to craft that you knew as a maker.

Do you think that part of the struggle is that when you become a leader you become more removed from direct ownership of the product?

I don't think that it's just ownership. It's about integrity, and how you're framing what those different roles mean. If I'm a maker, and you're not a maker, I'm better than you because I have integrity, and you don't. You're just talking. So it's about a necessary reframing of your "maker" role. You no longer get your hands dirty or clothes messed up as a badge of belonging. As a leader, you are alone—and accountable for the needs of the whole. The whole is the product. And you're making it. You own it. And you succeed and fail by it.

Does this relentless focus on integrity have an upside when it comes to leading a business?

I think the pursuit of integrity is a good thing, because it isn't about profit—it's only about quality. Companies need a very clear sort of compass to succeed, and when profit is the motivation, it isn't enough. Creatives are driven by passion, by integrity, and by quality. So they know how to focus on product, and how it feels. And that's a very important strength. Especially right now. It used to be that you would buy a product just because it had good technology. You didn't care about the design. But that's not the case anymore.

I know a lot of founders who get discouraged as they move into management because they're less involved in the day-to-day making. Have you had that feeling as the focus of your work has shifted?

I guess I don't internalize that kind of romanticism. But I do know many people like that. They've built a business and don't make anymore, and they're kind of unhappy.

I think that true creative leaders recognize that they live and die by their team. For example, when I first sat with Jony Ive, Apple's senior VP of design, I recall how proud he was of his team. That's all he could talk about. He spoke about making his team with the same pride you would normally only see in the Apple TV commercials where the aluminum is being milled to micro-millimeter precision. There's a craft to making a team, and creative leaders take pride in that craft.

Is embracing leadership really just a question of reframing how we see it?

Creative people are good at inspiring others. So in theory, they are good at leading. But they so want to make. After I took the job as president of the Rhode Island School of Design in 2008, people were always coming to me and saying, "Oh, you must be so sad you aren't making art. Oh, you poor thing, etc., etc." And my response has always been, well, I'm making a different kind of thing now.

I'm getting to participate in making the STEAM Movement, which is working to make art and design a central part of education and innovation in America. I'm also working to make the impact of design and tech working together more visible in Silicon Valley. So I'm still making—I'm just making something different. I'm participating in making communities, and learning a lot in the process, the same way I would get to learn while making things on the computer.

Only now the timeline is longer. A lot longer. You don't get the immediate gratification that you might as a designer when the timelines are shorter. But artists are used to delayed gratification. I look at the work I do now as a new kind of art.

Do you think that creatives have this attitude toward leadership—like it's something "less than"—because it's just not part of the curriculum that we learn? That we're never taught that it's important or valuable?

I think it's easy to put leadership down, like it doesn't matter. But one thing I've realized is that every field has its own heroes. If you're thinking of design, you have Paul Rand. If you think of business, you have Peter Drucker. If you think of technology, you have an Andy Grove or a Steve Jobs. And if you think of leadership, there are heroes as well, like John Gardner, the brilliant author of *On Leadership and Self-Renewal*, or Marshall Ganz, whose teachings about personal narratives have inspired me greatly. I frequently give reading lists to people who want to understand that there is a field called "leadership," and once they discover the work that these people have done, they can see that there is a certain creativity and truth and integrity to leadership.

It seems like, in theory, the ideal leader would be a maker, a manager, and a leader. Do you think that those things all coexist in one person with any kind of frequency?

I don't know about frequency, but I know about growth and how people evolve. Given the current environment, I think that people are being forced to change. A few decades ago, when things were more stable, we could all just sort of stay in our little roles. But now the pace of change is so rapid, and things are confusing. So we have to just try stuff. And fail. And recover, and try again. If there's one skill that a leader needs, it's the attitude espoused by the late, great Nelson Mandela, "Do not judge me by my successes; judge me by how many times I fell down and got back up again." Creatives know that attitude so well—and manage ambiguity better than anyone else. And combined with the ability to execute, to really get things done, they're in a great position to lead.

JOHN MAEDA is design partner at Kleiner Perkins Caufield & Byers, where he works with KPCB's entrepreneurs and portfolio companies to build design into their company cultures. He also chairs the eBay Design Advisory Council. You can follow him on Twitter @johnmaeda.

→ www.creativeleadership.com

"The more one does,

the more one can do."

COMMUNICATING FOR SPEED, CLARITY, AND INNOVATION

—

William Allen

One of the greatest drains on a company's resources is a lack of clarity and direction. No matter how fast a runner you are, if you're running in the wrong direction, you'll never win the race. Great leaders know this. If your business's strategy and goals aren't communicated clearly—both from you to your team and internally among the team members themselves—you will waste the most precious resource you have: time.

But how do you establish a culture that supports great communication? Given that we live in an era in which our communication channels have proliferated wildly, the easy answer is to assume that it will just take care of itself. And yet the opposite is actually true.

THE COMMUNICATION PARADOX

Organizations today are flatter and less hierarchical than ever before. The tasks that most knowledge workers undertake are increasingly self-directed, a key factor in employee retention, performance, and overall happiness. Internal teams are created, reorganized, and disbanded with remarkable speed, a necessity when building for a future no one has seen.

This is good news, of course. The disappearance of hierarchy and the emergence of rapid iteration are essential to competing in a rapidly changing world. Ideas—that base ingredient for innovation—quickly disseminate in flat organizations, increasing the chances for creating something new, better, more innovative.

Yet the teams that adopt this new style of work face a number of challenges. When the makeup of your team is constantly changing, you lose the continuity and institutional knowledge so important to maintaining quality and consistency. When the individuals on your team are evolving the roles they play, more time and effort can go into getting them up to speed versus actually fulfilling their duties. Without the clear direction that some forms of hierarchy enable, teams can struggle to work on projects that are relevant to the overall strategy.

In other words: even though we live in an era where we communicate and collaborate with incredible fluidity, we must work harder than ever as leaders to make sure that everyone is on the same page.

CREATE REDUNDANCY, REPEAT YOURSELF CONSTANTLY

Never assume your team knows the outcomes of the decisions you make on a daily basis. Assuming—instead of actively informing—guarantees they will spend more time guessing what they should be doing versus actually doing it. To ensure that you're regularly communicating both the big picture and the reasoning behind daily decisions, here are a few tactics you can use:

- **Have a colleague join you in all of your meetings (and it doesn't have to be the same one for every meeting).** Empower him or her to inform the rest of the team about the key decisions that were made and how it impacts the business's direction.

- **Repeat yourself.** You likely spend your days talking to a number of different audiences. While repeating the same message might feel tedious, it's essential for your message to be heard. Remember: even if you're repeating yourself dozens of times a day, each person that you collaborate with is hearing it once, at best.

- **Err on the side of openness.** Many leaders are shocked to find out the degree to which their teams already know something is happening, even if the details are murky. Rumors of a big new client, layoffs, bonuses, or any important decision can disseminate widely before any details emerge. Preempt this by being as transparent as possible as early as possible.

GIVE YOUR TEAM TOOLS TO TALK

Even if you do all of the above, outbound communication from the leadership has its limits. Equally important is ensuring your team members make a habit of communicating effectively among themselves. A few ideas:

Host a TED Conference, but just for you. At Behance, we frequently host internal "sneak previews," where a small project team will give everyone a demo of what they're working on and explain how it relates to the business's broader mission. This sort of forum encourages individual teams to take a leadership role and show off their expertise, while engendering a deeper understanding of how their work fits into the overall strategy.

Hold weekly "all-hands" meetings. Creating a ritual for regularly clarifying what everyone is working on (and how it impacts others) is crucial. Try holding a weekly all-hands meeting, where each team can quickly inform everyone else about key upcoming activities. These can and should be standing meetings (i.e., no one sits) that last fifteen minutes or less, with more in-depth, one-on-one discussions taking place off-line. The goal is to unearth new dependencies and quickly get on the same page so you can move faster toward your goals.

Keep a public record of what everyone is doing. The engineering team at Behance convinced the rest of us to use a group chat program—Slack in our case—and we can no longer imagine life without it. The ability to have publicly recorded interactions among an entire team that don't require being in the same room at the same time—and to split off into deeper dives through private chat—is the single best way we've found to keep everyone aware of what's happening.

Leverage technology, but don't force it. Mix and match the technology that best works for you, whether it's a project management app, a group messaging program, or even the generous use of Post-it notes and whiteboards. But be wary of dictating the technology your team uses: broad adoption is more important than any specific feature set. Better to build off what your team naturally gravitates toward rather than forcing the "perfect" solution.

Favor in-person conversations over e-mail. All of us have become too reliant on written communication, and perhaps too reliant on its ability to delay making important decisions. A few minutes of face-to-face conversation can often eliminate days of back-and-forths via e-mail. My colleagues Zach and Jackie coined the word "FaceMail" for the age-old act of walking over to your colleague's desk and starting a conversation. Sometimes the oldest technology is still the best.

Use your physical space to encourage new conversations. The jury is out on whether the benefits of open-plan office spaces are worth their cost in productivity. But one thing is for sure: you communicate more frequently with those in close physical proximity to you. Exploit this fact by switching up your seating chart a few times a year. Move your designers closer to marketing. Have sales sit next to engineering. Informal communication (and idea exchange) is often a product of happenstance—so engineer that to your advantage.

When it stops working, stop doing it. The single worst reason to continue doing something is because you did it before. When a system or process starts to show signs of strain, ask what it was originally designed to solve and whether that problem still exists. If the problem no longer exists, scrap the process. If it does, refactor your process to make it work again.

How we work is changing, and that shift brings a number of benefits: more meaningful work, deeper collaboration, and faster innovation. But none of these things matter if you and your team aren't on the same page. Overcome the communication paradox, and you'll already be one step ahead of everyone else.

WILLIAM ALLEN is the senior director of Behance. He acted as Behance's COO prior to its acquisition by Adobe. Previously he created strategic partnerships with global brands at TED and was co-founder of the consultancy Industry Digital Media.

→ Follow him on Twitter @williamallen

"The only people who can change the world are people who want to."

— HUGH MACLEOD

BUILDING A TEAM OF LEADERS, NOT FOLLOWERS

—

David Marquet

When I think about human acts of greatness, it strikes me that there are two characteristics that distinguish them. First, these acts are always in the service of others, not ourselves. Whether it's a fireman entering a burning building, a waiter shielding dining guests from a terrorist's bullets, or a lifeboat operator returning to save people from a stricken vessel, acts of greatness are for others.

The second thing is that acts of greatness are never ordered. You could not order people to do the kinds of things they do when achieving great deeds. As a result, we have a serendipitous view of these acts.

We don't expect them, and we don't count on them. If someone in our midst does something great, we look on with admiration.

I believe all humans have the potential for acts of greatness. I call it the everyday superhero within. Unfortunately, fear, intimidation, posturing, and deception suppress the desire for people to embrace their potential. This is the case in most work places today where 70 percent of workers are disengaged and just want to make it through the day without making mistakes. This mind-set of avoiding errors rather than achieving greatness biases people toward inactivity, reactiveness, disengagement, and dissatisfaction.

But wouldn't it be amazing if we could somehow encourage acts of greatness? Not order them, but create an environment where people feel they can embrace the superhero within and achieve great things?

I think it's possible.

CREATING AN ENVIRONMENT OF TRUST

Human behavior is a combination of how a person's instincts nudge them (let's call it personality) and how the environment pushes them. Our hardwired tendency is to overweight the importance of personality and underweight the importance of the environment. In a toxic environment, everyone is capable of evil acts. In the right environment, everyone is capable of great acts. Our job as leaders is to shape the environment because we cannot reform personalities.

What does that environment look like? It starts with trust and a feeling of safety and connection. When I say *trust*, I mean something different than what you are probably thinking. Trust does not mean agreement that you, the manager, are always right or know best, but trust does mean that we are in it together and that you make decisions that optimize outcomes for the group as a whole. In other words, if you say there's a pink elephant behind me, I believe that you believe there is a pink elephant behind me. Whether or not there is a pink elephant behind me is not an issue of trust; it's a condition of the physical world.

Since acts of greatness cannot be ordered or coerced, the degree to which we order people around and provide them with explicit instructions may suppress any chance of greatness. The fundamental objective of leadership then is to create environments built on trust, where people practice winning at taking responsibility, winning at making decisions, and winning at taking action. Leadership is not about a manager making great decisions and issuing great orders, as I once thought.

This is that story.

WHY TELLING PEOPLE WHAT TO DO DOESN'T WORK

"Make all preparations to get under way," I ordered the second in command of the USS *Santa Fe*, a nuclear-powered submarine, in a bold and confident tone. "Make all preparations to get under way, aye, aye, sir." He acknowledged the order and went off, issuing subsequent commands and making things happen. Several hours later, I ordered the engineer to start up the reactor. Then, when all preparations had been made and the tugboat tied up alongside the submarine, I directed the officer of the deck (OOD), who orders the submarine's course, speed, and depth, to "get under way." The ship slipped away from the pier, and we headed down the main Pearl Harbor channel toward the Pacific Ocean. "Submerge the ship!" and we sunk beneath the surface. "Ahead flank!" and the *Santa Fe* surged ahead, deep in the sea. The crew was all too eager to please their new captain, and that was exactly the problem.

I had just taken command of the *Santa Fe*, a nuclear-powered submarine. It was January 1999. This was unplanned. For the past year, I had been preparing to take command of a different submarine model, one that was somewhat older. At the last minute, the captain departed abruptly and I was reassigned to the *Santa Fe*.

As I thought about taking command of the *Santa Fe*, I wanted to be a leader who empowered his subordinates, but the submarine was not performing well. People were doing what they were told, initiative was nonexistent, and fear of making mistakes paralyzed most decision makers into inaction. People were working in isolation. Plagued with poor morale and operational problems, almost every sailor who could was leaving the navy. Only three sailors from a crew of 135 the previous year reenlisted, and retention was at the bottom of the fleet. Officers were resigning their commissions, and the previous captain had quit. Based on my leadership training, I set about "inspiring and empowering" my men, upholding high standards of professionalism and extolling the benefits of teamwork. As we prepared to go to sea for the first time, I found myself issuing orders, commanding in the way I knew how. It was awesome and heady. I was acting solidly in the image of great leaders, or so I thought, confidently walking the ship and telling a compliant crew what to do.

The next day, it all changed.

We ran an exercise where we intentionally shut down the nuclear reactor to test our ability to find and correct faults. In the control room, the OOD was the officer with the longest time on board, and he was doing all the right things. We had shifted propulsion from the main engines to a backup motor. The backup can only power the ship at low speed and draws down the battery. During the long trouble-shooting period while the nuclear technicians were isolating the fault, I started thinking things were going too smoothly. I couldn't let the crew think their new captain was easy!

Since I was assigned to the *Santa Fe* at the last minute, I wasn't the technical expert that I would have been had I gone to my originally assigned submarine. As a result, I did what no captain of a nuclear submarine should ever do—I made a mistake. I suggested to the OOD that he order something that was not possible at the time—to speed up on the backup motor. The startling thing was that he immediately ordered it. Fortunately, it was not carried out by the crew. The OOD later told me that he knew it wasn't executable but ordered it anyway because I "told him to." I realized that we had a crew that was trained for compliance, and a captain trained for the wrong submarine. If we didn't fix that, it could prove to be a disaster.

USING LANGUAGE TO INSTILL OWNERSHIP AND RESPONSIBILITY

The officers and I gathered in the wardroom to discuss how we were going to survive my command tour, scheduled for the next three years. We decided that we would flip the typical leadership paradigm. Instead of "taking control, making followers," I would "give control, create leaders." From then on, I stopped giving orders and had the officers state their intentions with "I intend to . . ." and I would respond with "Very well." This was a departure from the standard practice of "requesting permission" for events and operations by the officers and the captain ordering them. In addition to creating ownership in the mind of the officer, they all had to think like the captain. Saying "I intend to . . ." released a torrent of passion and initiative. Not only did it result in immediate performance improvements; it proved powerful in the long run. Ten of those *Santa Fe* officers were subsequently selected to command submarines.

I learned that if you want people to think, telling them what to do is not the best way to do it—in fact, it's the worst.

We found dozens of examples where the way we did business sent the signal that people were supposed to do what they were told, and, thus, they were absolved of responsibility. It turns out that if your leadership is based on the belief that there are only two kinds of people in the world—leaders and followers—empowerment is just a Band-Aid for the fact that you've turned your people into followers. Once treated like followers, people act like followers. It saps their passion and initiative.

In the military, we love briefings. In a briefing, the boss tells people what is going to happen and what is expected of them. We think this is helpful, but only so in a top-down way. A brief is an active event for the briefer but passive for everyone else. Members "are briefed." In other words: show up; we'll tell you what to do. Recognizing this limitation, we eliminated all briefs on board the *Santa Fe* and replaced them with certifications where the junior officers and sailors reported their anticipated actions to a senior officer. That senior officer weighed the depth of the responses and decided whether or not the team was ready to conduct the event. Thus a certification was different from a briefing in two key ways: first, it was active for the entire team, not passive; second, it was a decision point.

The *Santa Fe* performed superbly while I served as its captain. The release of intellectual power, distributed decision making, and passion were overwhelming. Within a year we went from worst to first in almost all operational measures. Even though from my point of view people were working harder and thinking harder than they were before, retention skyrocketed. We went from three reenlistments the previous year to thirty-three reenlistments. That put us at the top of the fleet. What was special, however, was that the leadership structure embedded the "goodness" of what we did in the people and practices of the submarine, which continued to do well long after my departure. Only ten years later can we assess the true success of that work—with the *Santa Fe*'s continued operational excellence and the implausibly high promotion rates for its officers and crew. This is the legacy of giving control, creating leaders.

~

I am guessing that, like me, you will feel discomfort as you give control to others. This is normal. I frequently failed to live up to the image I'd created for myself as a leader. I'd come down hard on myself and sulk, but this wasn't helpful behavior. Once I got over it, I was out there trying again and again. As you face these challenges, you will find your own kryptonite, you will struggle, and you will overcome. And your greatest achievement will be helping those around your embrace their inner superhero.

DAVID MARQUET *is the former commander of the nuclear-powered submarine USS* Santa Fe *and author of* Turn the Ship Around!

→ www.davidmarquet.com

KEY
TAKEAWAYS

—

Leading Your Team

Get more insights and the desktop wallpaper at:

→ www.99u.com/leading

STOP COMPLAINING AND START FIXING

Don't dismiss management; step into it (and give it a better name!). Adopt a "servant leader" approach and ask how you can help those around you become their best selves.

KEEP YOUR "MAKER" MIND-SET

Bring the same craft and attention to detail you have as a maker to the challenges of leadership—to building relationships, assembling a team, and guiding your product.

CHECK YOUR EGO AT THE DOOR

Rather than "taking control," strive to "give control" to your team members. Giving people ownership and responsibility sparks passion and initiative.

SHARE ALL THE INFORMATION, ALL THE TIME

Don't be afraid to share information broadly and repeat yourself constantly. It's always good to err on the side of over-communication to keep your team on track.

REFACTOR RELENTLESSLY

Reexamine the way your team is working at regular intervals—especially when you're growing rapidly. If a process isn't working anymore, scrap it and refactor immediately.

LET IT ALL HANG OUT

Experiment with transparency—whether it's sharing meeting notes, investor details, or even employee salaries. It's uncomfortable at first, but the benefits can be massive.

A CALL TO ACTION

—

A parting message on making the leap

ARE YOU READY?

—

Seth Godin

A friend asked her niece to pass a pitcher of water down the table. "Oh, no, Auntie," the three-year-old girl said. "I'm not nearly old enough or wise enough to do that."

"When will you be ready?" my friend asked.

The girl hesitated for a moment and said, "I'll be old enough in about thirty minutes."

How old will you be before you're ready?

We're never ready. Important stuff, innovations that matter, they always need a bit more time, because the market isn't quite ready for the leap we need it to take. The market isn't ready, and neither are we.

The first person who used Instagram—what exactly did he do with it? Of course the app was launched prematurely, because it didn't work unless you had other people to send pictures to. And the car was marketed before we had roads to drive on and gas stations to fill up with.

Alexander Graham Bell launched the telephone long before people knew how to use it or realized that they wanted one. His original plan was for people to answer by saying, "Ahoy," because there wasn't a socially acceptable way for the upper classes to initiate a conversation without being introduced first. Fortunately, his friend Thomas Edison coined the now overused term *hello*.

We tell people that the route to Carnegie Hall is paved with practice, practice, practice. But practice is another word for preparation.

I'm not talking about being prepared. Preparation isn't the same as ready. Ready is an emotional choice, the decision to put something into the world and say, "Here, I made this." The emotional choice of exposing ourselves and shipping the work. The paradox is obvious: the more important the idea, the less we can be ready.

And so we fret that the world, or our market, isn't ready for the leap. The world isn't ready for mixed-race couples, or gay marriage, or a woman CEO, we say. The market isn't ready for a $400 smartphone or e-books or a national brand of vegan ice cream, we say.

It's too soon, we say.

Everywhere we turn, the doors appear to be closed, not open. The market is now dominated by the famous. A few weeks ago, eight out of ten books on the *New York Times* bestseller list were either by TV personalities or had been turned into movies. We have created a culture where the best way to have a voice is to be famous, which of course means that you, you the person who's not yet famous, isn't ready to have a voice. It's not your turn, you're not ready.

Here's the thing: Every idea that matters hits the market too soon. While you're busy practicing and preparing, you're also hiding from the market, keeping your worthy and world-changing idea from the rest of us.

If you wait until you are ready, it is almost certainly too late.

SETH GODIN has written seventeen books that have been translated into more than thirty-five languages. Every one has been a bestseller. He writes about the post–Industrial Revolution, the way ideas spread, marketing, quitting, leadership, and, most of all, changing everything.

→ www.sethgodin.com

"Do I dare disturb the universe?"

— T. S. ELIOT

ACKNOWLEDGMENTS

—

My heartiest thanks must go to our absolutely amazing brain trust of contributors: William Allen, Rich Armstrong, Scott Belsky, Warren Berger, Sean Blanda, Neil Blumenthal, Craig Dalton, Jane ni Dhulchaointigh, Aaron Dignan, Andy Dunn, Joel Gascoigne, Seth Godin, Chris Guillebeau, Emily Heyward, John Maeda, David Marquet, Tim O'Reilly, Shane Snow, Sebastian Thrun, Keith Yamashita, and Julie Zhuo. This book would not exist without your insights and expertise. Thank you so much for your time, your energy, your patience, and your generosity. It's been an honor and a pleasure to work with all of you.

The aesthetics of this book owe a huge debt to Behance co-founder and chief of design Matias Corea, one of my favorite creative collaborators, and to Raewyn Brandon, who's the most talented young designer I know by a long shot. The beautiful cover design and the crisp interior layout—and the vision for how all three of the books in this series fit together—are entirely theirs. Much appreciation to you both for making my world, and this book, beautiful.

99U managing editor Sean Blanda has been an invaluable sounding board throughout the creation of this book—I couldn't have done it without him. In addition to being a wonderful ally and a great writer who I'm proud to include here, Sean gave me a few great ideas for contributors when I needed them most. Much thanks as well must go to our assistant editor Sasha VanHoven for helping me assemble a killer PR plan for the book and then executing on it across all of our 99U channels.

Amazon editor Katie Salisbury has been a wonderful (and patient) supporter throughout this process. Huge thanks to her for deft edits to smooth out the prose herein, and for posing great questions to push me to make this book even better. Many thanks as well to Anna Riego and Courtney Dodson for running a tight production schedule and keeping us organized and on track, as well as to the entire Amazon team for enthusiastically supporting and promoting this book and the entire 99U book series.

Lastly, I must extend much, much appreciation to Scott Belsky for his feedback and contributions to this book series and—most importantly—for giving me the freedom to helm such an amazing (and fun) project. Having the chance to lead 99U, and develop this book series, as part of Behance's mission to empower the creative world has been—and will continue to be—an incredible and invigorating opportunity for which I am deeply grateful.

— *JOCELYN K. GLEI, editor-in-chief, 99U*

ABOUT 99U

—

99U is Behance's effort to deliver the "missing curriculum" that you didn't get in school, highlighting best practices for making ideas happen. We do this through interviews, articles, and videos on our Webby Award–winning website at 99u.com, our annual 99U Conference in New York City, our bestselling book *Making Ideas Happen*, and our ongoing 99U book series, which includes *Manage Your Day-to-Day*, *Maximize Your Potential*, and this book, *Make Your Mark*.

→ *www.99u.com*

ABOUT THE EDITOR

—

As editor-in-chief and director, Jocelyn K. Glei leads 99U in its mission to provide the "missing curriculum" on making ideas happen. She oversees the 99u.com website—which has won two Webby Awards for Best Cultural Blog—and leads the curation and execution of the popular 99U Conference, which has presented talks from visionary creatives including Jack Dorsey, Beth Comstock, Brené Brown, Jonathan Adler, Stefan Sagmeister, Jad Abumrad, and many more. She is also the editor of the 99U book series, which includes *Manage Your Day-to-Day*, *Maximize Your Potential*, and this book, *Make Your Mark*.

Prior to joining Behance and 99U, Jocelyn was the global managing editor at the online media company Flavorpill, leading development of new editorial products. She has also consulted with dozens of brands and agencies, from Herman Miller to PSFK to Huge, Inc., on content strategy and web launches. She is passionate about creating editorial products that people love.

→ *www.jkglei.com*

INDEX

—